LIFE HISTORY OF DAVID F. (DAVE) HART

Copyright © 2022 David F. Hart All rights reserved. No part of this book may be reproduced in any form or by any electronic or mechanical means, including information storage and retrieval systems, without written permission from the publisher.

Library of Congress Cataloging-in-Publication Data available

ISBN 979-8-9872611-0-1 (hardcover)
ISBN 979-8-9872611-1-8 (e-book)

∞™ The paper used in this publication meets the minimum requirements of American National Standard for Information Sciences—Permanence of Paper for Printed Library Materials, ANSI/NISO Z39.48-1992

Printed in the United States of America

FOREWORD

by Shane Hart, son

A few important points as you start this book:

A majority of this book was written sometime between November 28, 1976 and February 9, 1977 when my dad was thirty-four years old. He hadn't yet lived half of his life, but his writing at that time comprises 78% of the words in this book. With most of this account over forty-five years old at this time, you will feel startled at certain things you read unless you remember when it was written and at what stage of life my dad was in. The good news is that most of these memories were recorded when they were fresher and more recent. The bad news is that you miss out on some of Dad's wisdom and some of his experiences since that time. I think it goes without saying that if Dad wrote his full life history today, some things would be emphasized and written about differently. But fortunately...

An update was hand-written in 2019 and is included in this book in *italicized font*. The *italicized font* portion is still a few years old, but it gives you some additional insights and information from Dad's life, even if not all of it is totally up-to-date. As I mentioned above, though, the *italicized font* portion comprises a minority of this book even though it covers more years. So the updates are at a little higher level and not as detailed as his previous writing. The two accounts are combined in the way that makes the most sense given the material's structure.

The most important thing I want everyone reading this to know is this: **My dad is the greatest.** He is the absolute best. I could not think more highly of him or love him more. And I really hope you do, too–especially after reading his life history. Let me explain why Dad is the greatest, and then maybe I can use it as his eulogy someday. (If you know Dad, that way of thinking comes straight from him–both the planning for his funeral, which he has already done, and being efficient with work in a way that it accomplishes more than one purpose.)

My dad is the most honest person that I know. If on the rare occasion you find him telling even a half-truth, you will see Dad squirm with an internal wrestling of his conscience that is almost comical, until he finally lets out the full truth in a burst of relief. I remember being just over the age of twelve and Dad taking me to the movies (in my mind, I recall it was "Hoosiers"). Knowing that he would save $1 on my ticket if the cashier thought I was under twelve years of age, he went up to the ticket window and said, "One Adult and one Child, please." As the cashier took the money and started to unspool the tickets, Dad squirmed and squirmed until he could no longer take it. Seconds later, without any question or hesitation on the part of the cashier, he admitted I was twelve and paid the extra $1.

Dad might be the kindest person I know. Throughout my life I've heard Dad think the best of almost any person or individual. He gives people the benefit of the doubt. He tries to lift others. In this book, Dad writes, "I have always worked at being well-liked. I've tried to do the things that people would approve of and tried hard not to offend others." A lifetime of working to be liked has made him an incredibly friendly individual.

Dad is very, very patient. It took me many years to get him riled up to the point where he gave me the worst beating he ever gave to any of us kids. But I was determinedly troublesome as a child and eventually I wore him down. It would take any other father or person weeks or, at best months, before they snapped in the same way. I'm half-kidding about this, by the way. It's one of those family stories that we retell with my siblings. But trust me–and I'm sure others already know, as I've heard Jan say it many times–those who have tried his patience have seen just how long Dad can extend it. And his patience is impressive.

Dad is a very fun person to be around. Dad is extremely comfortable with himself which makes it easy to spend time with him. He is meek, but not in a weak or submissive way. He endures injury, mistreatment from others, or life's trials without resentment and with minimal angst, (which takes great strength). He tells it like it is, so you always know where he stands and what he thinks. And just as he wrote, he always strives to avoid mistreating or offending others. If he does offend someone, he thinks very hard about where he went wrong, determines to do better in the future, and then he leaves his mistake in the past. And if he has offended someone without committing a mistake, he lets it go without beating himself up over it or needlessly worrying. For someone who is anxious for a different outcome, he is incredibly low-key about it when someone is offended or doesn't like him.

I'm also of the opinion that **Dad is the most well-balanced person I know.** Sometimes it seems like he is like a walking dichotomy. In reality, he maintains an incredibly healthy balance in nearly every aspect of life. And it takes a healthy balance to navigate the realities of day-to-day living. No one does it better than Dad. Let me give some examples to illustrate:

My Dad is ~~cheap~~ economical. Another family story: At one point when it was us four kids living with just Dad, my sister Heidi needed a new bra. Dad had never bought clothes for himself at this stage in life, let alone having purchased something like a bra for someone else. Knowing how economical Dad is, my sister automatically went right for the least expensive one on the department store rack. When she presented it to Dad, though, he nearly made this book much shorter by having a heart attack.

"TWELVE DOLLARS?!?!?" he shouted out. The whole department store turned to look at us. I slid away to put some distance between us and hid behind a rack of clothes where no one could see me. Poor Heidi had to stand there while he repeatedly said, "TWELVE DOLLARS?!?! YOU'VE GOTTA BE KIDDING ME! TWELVE DOLLARS?!?!" Heidi pointed out that it was the cheapest one. Dad fixed his eye on a button-sized bow glued on between the cups and said, "Well what if we got rid of this fancy bow? Does that lower the price?" Dad inspected the rack of bras closely and failed to find a lesser price. Defeated, and after hearing the saleswoman (who joined the rest of the store and me in feeling mortified for Heidi) tell him that it was the most inexpensive one, he started to reach for his wallet. Slowly and painfully he paid, repeating sentences like, "I can't believe it," or "That's a lot of money for a little cloth."

And yet, **Dad is also very generous.** One time my wife, daughter, and I were going to the zoo with him. The zoo used to have free admission for many years but now they were charging $7 a ticket. Dad repeated (on a much smaller, quieter scale) the same behavior as when he bought Heidi the bra: "Seven dollars?! You've gotta be kidding me! I can't believe it! They charge seven dollars now?" And yet halfway through our walk in the zoo he put a wad of cash in the pocket of my jacket to cover the costs of our tickets. When you know how much it hurts him to spend, you easily see how very generous he is with those he cares about. He walks the line between being economical and giving very well.

Another line that he walks quite well is the one between being a father and being a friend. Next to my wife, I would call Dad my best friend, except that I wouldn't want to show any disrespect to his role as a father. You'll read in this book a story of when his father (my grandpa) slapped Dad for showing disrespect. I can think of a similar experience I had. Dad started wearing a new hairstyle once when I was in high school. Instead of his hair moving directly sideways each way from the part, it kind of swept backwards first. I jokingly referred to him as "Big Wave Dave" to someone and Dad found out about it. He angrily pulled me aside. He didn't care anything about my comment on his hairstyle. But he was very upset that I called him "Dave." I remember him shaking a finger in my face and nearly yelling, "You call me 'Dad'! You show me respect!" I've reflected on how perfect a response it was ever since. And I've learned that, first and foremost, **I respect Dad as the best father ever.** In a very close second, **I love him as almost my best friend.**

One final story to illustrate how well-balanced Dad is: At Dad's retirement party, he actually requested to be roasted, (like a comedy roast, where people make fun of the guest of honor). You can't believe how much fun all of his long-serving employees enjoyed retelling stories, making each other laugh at his expense, and poking fun at Dad. I know my siblings and I thoroughly enjoyed it as well. There was a tremendous

FOREWORD

amount of laughter all evening. You might not believe who enjoyed it the most, though: Dad.

Dad might have laughed the loudest and longest of all. He had the event recorded and watched it many times–laughing again and again–over the next several days. I don't think he was offended by a single thing said about him or a single joke made at his expense. I marveled then, and I have marveled many times since, at his unshakeable self-belief. **Dad is the most confident person I know.** And yet who else could be humble enough to not just endure being made fun of, but to invite it and welcome it? That takes some strength. Dad knows how to walk the fine line between confidence and humility.

Since this book captures Dad's memories of so many of you, I feel I should add one final story just in case his memories of you or his memories of a particular situation that involve you are not 100% accurate. (It is human nature that our memories are never perfect.) One day, my sister Jackie and I were talking with Dad, who mentioned off-hand that he was sorry that we weren't able to appreciate his excellent sense of humor, because he had to be our father first and because his sense of humor had diminished a little over time. To prove his point Dad told us that he had been voted by his classmates "Best Sense of Humor" in the senior superlatives. (This is something he reaffirms in the Personal Profile section of this book writing, "I was voted the 'most humorous' by my classmates which was very satisfying to me.")

Jackie and I jokingly (to some extent) pretended like we didn't believe it. The more we protested that it couldn't be true, the more Dad held firm, finally insisting that we go in the house and look at his high school yearbook. I think at this point we were ready to let it go –and frankly, I was starting to believe that it really was true. But because he was so enthusiastic to prove his point, we followed him inside where he took out the Preston High School 1960 yearbook. He flipped some pages before stopping to exclaim, "There! It's right there! See … 'Best Sense of Humo … oh.' Malin Davis. Well–Malin WAS hilarious …"

Dad is the best.

CONTENTS

Childhood	1
Education	7
School Activities (non-athletic)	13
Idaho Army National Guard	17
Where I've Lived	21
Update on Where I've Lived written 2019, age seventy-seven years old	29
Courtship	35
Update on Courtship written in 2020, age seventy-seven years old	45
Employment	61
Update on Employment written in 2019, age seventy-seven years old	73

Family	77
Update on Family written in 2019, age seventy-seven years old	89
Athletics	97
Update on Athletics written in 2019, age seventy-seven years old	119
Coaching	123
Personal Profile	135
Church	139

CHILDHOOD

I was born the third child of Marcus and Clara Walburger Hart on April 14, 1942 in Kirkland, Washington. Kirkland is a part of Seattle, as is Bothell, where my dad was teaching band at Bothell High School. I spent my first three years there, but as is typical of my memory, I don't remember one thing from those years. The family moved to Preston, Idaho where my father had been raised. There, my father taught school for several years. He taught band for a time, taught seminary, and taught one year of business education before going into business for himself.

The thing I remember about my earlier years more than anything is the neighborhood we played in and my friends there. All the kids we grew up with lived slightly less than a block east of our home. On one half of a block there were about six families, all with many young children. It was a natural place for us to find someone to play with. We had nine kids in our family. Besides the nine kids, our home offered a special attraction: an orchard which included several varieties of apple trees, (yellow transparent being our favorite), pear trees, (two varieties), and I also recall we had sugar plums, gooseberries, and raspberries. We also had, in those earlier years, a chicken coop and many chickens. The only thing between our home and the others in the neighborhood to the east was an alfalfa field. It was, needless to say, an ideal place to grow up.

The neighbors who were closest to my age, and for whom I have very special feelings, were Cyril and Sherry McKenzie, Coleen and Ronnie Hunt, Deverl, Karen, and Bud Cutler, Ralph and Doug Brenchley, and Jan and Randy Eberhard. There were two other families also, but I didn't feel quite as close to them as to these.

We spent a great deal of our time playing the usual games of hide-and-seek, "pom-pom-pullaway," and "Run, Sheep, Run." One of our biggest activities was playing in a hole which had been dug for a foundation of a house, but for some reason the foundation was never poured. We used to build "fox holes" and spend endless hours playing military games (which meant taking turns sneaking up on the fox holes we made, as carefully as possible, or else giving our all-out charge in "kamikaze" fashion. I guess the whole point of the game was to see how "neat" you could die when you were shot.)

CHILDHOOD

We also spent thousands of hours in the "hollow." Adjacent to our house on the south was a ravine, or hollow, that ran east for about half-a-mile and then ran north and south for several miles. The hollow had a creek in the bottom (I guess it was actually more of an irrigation ditch) that was quite muddy. It was a natural place to hunt for snakes and frogs. There was also a flume that carried a large ditch of water across this hollow. It was supported by large, interlacing poles much taller and about the same width as telephone poles. We used to walk and even run across this flume, stepping from 2"x 4" to 2"x 4", which were about five feet apart. At the highest point above the ground the flume was probably 120' to 150' high. I would never let my children play on it, but we kids spent hours on it. I would guess I've crossed it over a hundred times. It's amazing, but I don't think anyone ever got seriously hurt on it. The worst thing I saw was an older kid running across, and a 2"x 4" broke under his weight and he fell into the water.

I guess we spent 95% of our pre-school time, spare time, and summers in one of those two areas (neighborhood and hollow). I spent very little time doing anything other than playing with my friends. I can't remember doing anything with my family except coming home for meals and to go to sleep when it got dark or when everyone else had to go in. My parents raised us in a very unstructured manner. The only guidelines I can recall were that we were not to do bad things like steal, swear, or smoke, and we were cautioned about the dangers of drowning and even occasionally about the danger of the flume. (We were careful on the flume.) When I got hungry, I'd go home and mother would fix me something to eat. I couldn't play with my friends because they were called in to eat. I would guess that during the summer there were four things that were staples in our diet: Mother's brown bread, bananas, grapes, and watermelon. Usually with these items we'd have garden vegetables. The Harts used to think the neighbors' white bread was super–the next best thing to eating cake. Conversely, the neighbors used to love to eat Mrs. Hart's brown bread! (The grass is always greener …)

I vividly recall one incident from my younger days. Mr. Nelson, who owned the alfalfa field between our place and the vacated foundation hole, one day swore at my older brother and sister and a few of their friends for running across his field. I decided I'd show him and stick up for those in the field. While hiding in the hole, I shouted out every bad word I could think of and told Mr. Nelson off. Mr. Nelson wanted to know who it was that cursed him so badly. Then I really got scared. I ran out of the hole and hid so that he couldn't find me. I was really afraid to go home because his house was the next house to the north of us. He would surely see me. I couldn't go home by way of the hollow (to the south) because it was so open. So I finally walked six blocks out of my way, and I circled east and north and west and south and east again to get back home without him seeing me. After I'd been home a short while, Mr. Nelson came over and told Mom and Dad what I'd done and asked them if he could take me over to his place to punish me. My folks told him they'd take care of it, and so he left. I was the hero that day to the older kids for standing up to Mr. Nelson, and my parents were hero figures also for saving me from "mean Mr. Nelson."

All-in-all, my childhood, as I recall it, was a great experience. I had very little trauma and an awful lot of fun and fond memories. My childhood, as the rest of my life thus far, was a fulfilling experience, and one marked by little, if any, regret.

EDUCATION

I started grade school in Preston and attended there until the middle of the fifth grade when we moved to Logan. We moved, I think, because Dad was working three days a week as a temple officiator. His vocabulary book business was starting to grow at that time, too, and he thought he would like to make it without teaching. He ended up working part time at a music store, and I'm sure those were the least comfortable times, financially-speaking, that we ever had. (Not that we suffered a lot, however.) In the spring of the seventh grade, we moved back to Preston, and I finished my schooling there.

Until we moved to Logan, I think my schooling found me undistinguished. What notoriety I had was due to the fact that every year in school we had to have diphtheria vaccinations, and every year, without exception, shortly after I had my shot, I fainted. After the first couple of years, my classmates all kept an eye on me to see the fun. The first time it happened (in the first grade) the teacher and the nurse had to catch me to get the needle in. After I sat down at my desk, I fainted and fell against an extremely hot radiator which burned my right cheek and my right hand and wrist in several places. Fortunately, the burn scars on my cheek were not too bad, but the burn on my wrist left three scars that are still visible.

I also fainted once when I was too young to remember in the doctor's office. When I fell, I cut my index finger badly enough, somehow, that it severed a tendon. I've never been able to use the last joint of that finger since. It has never been a problem, however, in anything I've tried to do.

In the fourth grade I played the cornet in beginning band for part of the year. I can't remember anything I learned on the cornet and I only picked it as an instrument to play because it looked easy, with only three fingerings. One day I couldn't find the cornet I was using, so I took a clarinet. (Dad used to sell band instruments in the summer, so we had several at home.) I learned more on the clarinet in that one day than I had in several months on the cornet. I learned to play the lower scale and enjoyed it. After a while, I got bored with band, and so I repeatedly told the teacher that my reed was broken. One day the teacher asked me if he could see it, so when I got it out of the case, I hurried and split it with my fingernail so he wouldn't catch me. I had guilty feelings about

EDUCATION

my lack of interest in music, since all the Harts seemed so musical. But I really had no desire for it.

In elementary school, I was struck with the idea that eye glasses would be pretty neat to wear. We had a few students who had them, so at our annual testing for eyes, I faked the fact that I couldn't see the chart very easily. My parents were told that I needed glasses, so we went to Logan. The man who fitted me must have been as crooked as I was, because he fitted me with a pair of lenses that were like looking through a clean window. I wore my new glasses to school, but several kids made fun of them so I only wore them for a day or two at most.

In the seventh grade, my brother, Mark, was playing in a dance band, and I thought that was really cool. I told Mom that I wanted to take piano lessons so I could learn to play like Mark. I went to my first lesson and was so confused at what the instructor told me that I quit the same day, never to go back.

In Logan I took violin for half the year. I remember we played "Silent Night" for the Christmas cantata.

I also remember making a papier-mâché bird which was actually quite crummy, but it was a lot of fun to make, and I spent a lot of time doing it.

When I began attending Logan Junior High, there was a general class election and I was nominated to be vice president of the class. I made it through the primaries and ran against a very pretty girl (whom I later dated) in the finals. She won. It did a lot for my ego, however, as the new seventh grade class in the junior high was comprised of students from five elementary schools in the Logan area.

Occasionally, dances were held during the noon hour, but no one would dance. Many of the eighth grade girls wanted to dance but didn't dare ask their eighth grade boyfriends, so they asked us seventh grade boys. It never hurt my feelings that Mildred Cragun, a very popular girl who went with a very popular boy, asked me to dance. I thought that was alright.

At the beginning of the seventh grade, we were required to have a physical exam as part of the registration process. I think this was the first such exam I had ever had. The doctor informed me that I had a hernia (rupture) and that eventually I'd have to have an operation to correct it. He also said I couldn't participate in athletics until it was repaired. I was scared, to say the least, but we decided to have the operation three days after Christmas. The night before the operation I was so scared that I couldn't eat the good food they offered at the hospital. After I came out of the anesthesia, I was in a lot of pain the first day. I was given a hypo to help me sleep and to kill the pain. I think I knew what a heroin user must feel like. It was a super high feeling I'd get prior to going back to sleep. I was in the hospital for four days and was very sore and couldn't walk upright for eight to ten days.

When we moved back to Preston in March of my seventh grade year, I was really pleased with the super reception my old friends gave me. I was pleased to be back in Preston, although living in Logan had been a good experience.

EDUCATION

One of the earliest things I remember about my scholastic capabilities occurred in the ninth grade. We took a ninth grade math aptitude test. The highest students were placed in advanced algebra, the next in regular algebra, and the lowest in general math. I was put in the regular algebra class. This was the first time I thought that maybe I wasn't as smart as I had before assumed.

As a student, I was never concerned about getting A's, although I was very pleased when I got them. I was mostly concerned about not getting low grades. I didn't like C's, but I could live with them. I guess I basically tried to remain in the B-range. My worst grades came in my senior year when I sluffed twice to be with Kay and got caught both times. I was given 10% grade cuts for each sluff and received two D's as a result. These are the only grades I ever received below a C until I got past my master's degree. The only class I recall that I ever tried to get an A in was in my senior year and was taught by my football coach. I really wanted to impress him and not only got straight A's each quarter, but got the highest on each test he gave. My high school grade point average, I would guess, was probably about 2.8. My college grade point was 3.1, and I was much more conscientious about my studies there than I was in high school.

During my senior year in college I was selected as the Outstanding Male graduate from the Department of Physical Education. I was given a certificate and a pen and pencil set at a special College of Education program. Earlier, I had been elected the President of the Physical Education Major and Minors Club during my senior year. I'm sure this had a large role in my being selected for this honor. I had also been involved in the intramural program and had played freshman basketball for the Aggies.

The first three summers after graduation from USU, I returned to summer school and got my master's degree. This degree opened up the opportunity to go into either counseling or education administration with a little additional course work. I completed twenty semester hours of counseling course work after 1969 and am presently certified as a counselor with about six years of college education. With this education I have minors in History and driver education.

SCHOOL ACTIVITIES (NON-ATHLETIC)

During the ninth grade I was elected student body president of the Preston Junior High School. I don't recall doing anything with the position except presiding over student council. In the ninth grade I was also involved in a one-act play. I had the romantic lead and had to kiss a girl. I can imagine how frustrating it must have been to the director to get us to kiss, as we both acted so silly and made such a big deal about it. Most of my thespian activity was limited to one- or two-line parts. I think we put on a musical in the eighth grade and in that one I had one or two lines. I do remember that I got to wear a mustache, which I thought was pretty neat.

In the tenth grade, I joined the Thespian Club because a friend told me we didn't want to be nobodies and only have one picture in the yearbook. I probably had several parts, but they were so small I don't remember them. I know I was a policeman in "Arsenic and Old Lace."

During my junior year I was elected vice president of the class. I joined choir that year and enjoyed the trips we were able to take. In the musical "Carousel," I had another small part–you guessed it! I was a policeman and had one speaking line. Kay, incidentally, had the comedy lead in it. The Letterman's Club put on an assembly which was a take-off of the Ed Sullivan TV variety show. I was the MC and did a very poor imitation of Ed Sullivan. But everyone really enjoyed the job I did.

One of the highlights of my junior year was that Dad decided he was too busy to go back to Atlantic City, New Jersey, to the National Catholic Education Association Convention to sell his books, and I talked him into letting me go, rather than having no one go. Amazingly, he agreed. I left Ogden on a train and traveled clear across the country by myself. I had to make a train change in Chicago and catch a bus in Baltimore. When I arrived at the boardwalk on the oceanfront in Atlantic City, and after I checked into the hotel, I went to the convention center (where they hold the Miss America Pageant) and set up the materials for our booth.

I had a large felt sign representing the company, a table, and about four or five boxes of our vocabulary books. When I saw how many books we had (at least 300), I started worrying about getting rid of them all and what I'd do with them if I didn't get rid of them. I decided I'd never sell them, even at the half-price we were asking, so I made a sign that said, "Free Copies to English Instructors or Supervisors of English." After the first day, I had almost completely run out of books. I phoned Dad and told him what I'd done. He wasn't very happy with me. We decided I'd keep the few I had left and would show them to people. If they were interested, I'd have them fill out an order card and we'd send them one later in the mail. I don't know if any good came (for my dad) from my being at the convention, but it was a good experience for me.

The day before the convention ended, a man from Salt Lake City, who represented an electronics firm, saw that we were located in Preston, Idaho, where he had once lived. He stopped and talked to me and asked if I'd ever been to New York City. I said I hadn't and he said it would be a crime if anyone was as close as I was and didn't get up there. He said I could change or get credit for my return railroad trip in New York and I could ride with him there and he'd show me around. I went with him, and he drove me around the city for a couple of hours, showing me the sights. Then he took me to Penn Railroad Station and was going to drop me off. I asked him if he wouldn't come in just in case I had trouble and he did, although he didn't feel it was necessary. I was glad he did, because they wouldn't exchange my ticket and I only had about $8. The man from Salt Lake City wrote out a check for $30, with my promise that Dad would send him a check when I got home.

Besides being co-captain of the football team my senior year, I was elected vice president of the Boys League, which was a nothing organization consisting of all the boys in the student body. In the fall, I had a good part in the play "You Can't Take It with You," where I played the part of an eccentric ballet instructor. In the school musical "Showboat," I played "Joe," which had some speaking parts but was highlighted with a solo, "Old Man River," and another duet. Nothing makes me more nervous than singing alone. I really feel a lack of confidence and feel completely out-of-place. I believe I've only sung four solos in my life, to this point. We had a senior quartetwhich was pretty good. We won a superior (highest honor) at the district and regional music festivals. We also sang at several assemblies. One judge from Idaho State University told me I could come up and sing for him at ISU anytime. (I had no interest in singing any more than I already did.) At the end of my senior year, the student body voted on many different categories such as "Most Likely to Succeed," "Smartest," etc. I was voted "Best Athlete," tied for "Best All-around," and yes! "Prettiest eyes"! But as you would imagine, I was also voted "Most Handsome Boy"!

IDAHO ARMY NATIONAL GUARD

The summer before my senior year, I enlisted in the Idaho National Guard. We had a Howitzer Battery in Preston. I joined for two reasons: First, my brother Mark had joined and he thought it was alright. Second, the draft was a real possibility at that time, and I wanted to get married and finish school without the extended two years that being drafted in the army would require. I attended meetings twice a month and had an all-day drill once a month on a Sunday. The day after graduation from high school, nineteen of my classmates and I left the Salt Lake Airport on the worst-looking plane I have ever seen. It was my first flight, and the looks of the plane did nothing for my confidence. Upon arrival in Monterey,

California, we were bussed to Fort Ord, which is five miles away. We were immediately tasked with picking up some bedding and were assigned to some temporary barracks for our processing time. My name was called to go with a group which included no one I knew. I marched off, figuring I'd never see my friends again. I cried and was terribly homesick. A six-month commitment seems like an eternity when one is upset and unhappy. I was reunited with my friends, however, two days later, at the beginning of basic training.

There were many, many interesting and unique experiences in the service– too many to relate. The service was a great experience to have had, but very few ever want to go through it again. After basic, I went to clerk typist school. There was only one other friend from Preston with me there, but after the eight weeks of basic training, I was much better adjusted to army life. After the eight weeks of clerk typist school, the two of us were assigned to a company for six weeks where we did our on-the-job training.

While in the army, I went to San Francisco twice and to Los Angeles once. I had an Aunt Hazel, (Mother's sister), who lived in Salinas, which was fifteen miles inland. I used to spend Sundays with her family on many occasions.

Three particularly funny things happened at Fort Ord.

During basic training, we spent three weeks on the rifle range. When we shot the rifles, we had to do everything by the numbers. On command, a fellow would pick up a bullet. On command, he would hand it to me. On command, I would put it in the bore. On command, I would release the lever. On command, I'd aim, fire, etc. One day, after getting my bullet, I just slapped it in the bore and immediately released the lever preparing to aim. An officer standing behind me had been watching me progress on my own and he immediately pulled me from my hole and began chewing me out. Then he pulled all 200 men off the firing line and put them in company formation. He then proceeded to tell the whole company how I had figured I was better than the rest of them because I didn't need to follow orders and how I'd endangered all their lives. Then he ordered me to tell everyone, "I will load my weapon only on command." After I said that, he told me to yell louder. I did. Then he said, louder, and I screamed it out. He told me to keep it up, and in a matter of minutes, I lost my voice. Needless to say, I was extremely embarrassed and humiliated.

One day while we were in a huge open square with nothing but barren gravel under our feet and standing at attention, one of the soldiers ran about fifty yards straight out in front of us, crossed a paved road, and under one lone tree, pulled his pants down, and proceeded with his bowel movement. There he was, in plain sight of all 200 men in the company formation, seeking relief. He evidently had a serious case of diarrhea and had told his sergeant his problem. That was the only solution they could come up with.

The third incident happened when I was on KP, ("kitchen police," or "kitchen patrol"). In the room adjacent to the rear of the mess hall, a whole bunch of pies were stored. I told a friend of mine if he'd come around back, I'd steal a pie and he could take it up to our barracks and we'd eat it later. He agreed, so I took one when I felt I wouldn't be seen and gave it to him. On his way to the barracks he saw an officer approaching the same door he was entering, so he hurriedly slipped the pie inside his fatigue shirt and held it against his ribs with his arm as he approached the building. When he got up the stairs to our place, the crust had broken and cherry pie filling had soaked and stained his shirt, his belt, and the upper part of his pants.

So much for the army. I finished my military obligation in the middle of my senior year. I think it was a good way to have served, circumstances as they were.

WHERE I'VE LIVED

I was born in Kirkland, Washington, and spent my first three years in Bothell where Dad taught band and worked on his master's degree at the University of Washington. I remember nothing of living in Bothell.

Preston is where I consider myself to be from. I lived there from age three to age nine, and from age thirteen through age twenty. It was a great place to grow up. We had friends close to us, town was only four blocks away, and the wide-open spaces within a block of our house offered room to play. My ninth- grade year in school was the year Dad remodeled the house and made it a great place for bringing friends, and later, acquaintances. We owned enough land to have plenty of trees and garden space. For many years we had three huge poplar trees (we called them "giant") in our back yard. They were really awesome. One day I found a live porcupine in the middle of one of our lilac bushes at the side of our house. A neighbor came over and shot it with his .22 rifle and we dragged it off.

During a couple of years, I got into collecting baseball cards that came with bubble gum. I had them all organized into teams and built a box with a separate compartment for each team. I'm sure I had the best collection in Preston. There must have always been a card or two that they never printed just to keep a boy buying bubble gum. I remember Mickey Mantle was one of them.

Logan was pretty nice, but we were pretty well locked into the confines of the city. We lived at 271 East 300 North. We were close to Main Street and a block from the temple, but we were two or three miles away from the city limits. We'd play in the middle of the blocks and spent a lot of time there. The house we lived in was a fraternity house at one time. It was very big and was constructed of red brick. My grandmother, Ada Lowe Hart, lived in part of the house and I can remember her kindness. She showed us how to knit, gave us food, and read the Bible to us on occasion. There was a garage in the back with an attic. There we discovered an old phonograph with lots of old records which were all about 3/8ths of an inch thick. I'll bet they'd be worth a lot as collectors' items now.

I started collecting popsicle wrappers in Logan. With so many wrappers and a little money, I could get a hunting knife or hatchet, etc. Every nickel I got went for a popsicle, and I spent a great deal of the time walking gutters looking for wrappers, too.

When Dad would officiate at the temple, I often went up to play on the temple grounds and wait for him to get done so I could walk home with him.

The college (Utah State Agricultural College back then) was always a special attraction. Sometimes we'd go up there and see what was going on. We had a lot of fun sneaking into the football games by finding a dark part of the stadium and climbing the high-wire mesh fence.

I had several great friends during the school year, but during the summer I did not enjoy as many good friends. About half of these summer friends haven't turned out very well.

In my adult years, the first place I lived was Malad, Idaho. Malad was an old, sleepy town. When I lived there as a young, married man, there were only three or four couples we knew well who were reasonably close to our age. While living in Malad, we spent most weekends going to Logan, Ogden, Brigham City, or Salt Lake City to see movies or dine out. We usually went with the Budges or the Smiths with whom we associated a lot. I took up golfing with Wayne Budge and Gerald Williams and we went to Preston or Tremonton often to golf.

As I recall, my time in Malad was mostly spent in the pursuit of fun. I guess it is a natural reaction after one has struggled through school and finally is able to make some money. We bought a Chevrolet Impala Super Sport each of the first two years we lived there. We rented an old wood-frame home from Will McClurg, who was the oldest resident of Malad at the time. It cost us $50 a month. Mr. McClurg lived alone above us, and though he was in his nineties, he was pretty active. He could hardly hear, however. He used to spend evenings listening to Dodger baseball games with the volume turned so loud we could hear it downstairs. I liked Malad much more than Kay did. I was much more involved with my coaching. Kay couldn't get as involved and was unable to enjoy our home a great deal even though it was very decent for Malad standards.

When we moved to Soda Springs, we lived in a very nice apartment for $130 a month. Housing was very tight, and Superintendent Williams said we'd probably be better off buying a home. I told Kay we should wait a couple of years before making such a big investment, but she thought we should get right at it. We met some friends who helped us get a lot, select a house plan, and get a contractor. In March, we moved into our new home, although it wasn't quite finished. We did all the interior painting and had people come in to carpet it and lay linoleum, etc. It was one of the nicer homes in Soda and turned out to be a good investment and one of the very best decisions we ever made.

Soda became our home. The only thing we didn't like about Soda was the long, hard winters, which were usually compounded by a lot of wind. The nearest cities were Pocatello and Logan, seventy and eighty-five miles away, respectively, so we were secluded. Soda was a very progressive, new city, and we came to feel very much a part of it. We lived in an excellent location, half-a-block from the high school, half-a-block from the church, and only five blocks from town.

Soda is a real outdoor recreation area, and I came to thoroughly enjoy hunting ducks, geese, grouse, and doves in the fall. Occasionally I took in fishing with Mike and Evan Adams, our neighbor, at Blackfoot Reservoir. Mike and I used to go shooting the .22, usually at ground squirrels, which were numerous and a farmers' nuisance. Several times we went on picnics in the mountains. We also enjoyed just riding around the area.

Mike and I had some very special experiences together while hunting and fishing. When fishing, I usually hooked a fish and let Mike pull it in. One day he pulled in a three-and-a-half pound native trout. The fish were usually from two to two-and-a-half pounds. One day, I told Mike to watch the poles while I ran down to the inlet to look for geese. I had seen several flocks land there many times. I instructed Mike on what to do if the pole moved and told him I'd be back in ten minutes. I ran all the way so I wouldn't leave him alone very long. When I returned, he had pulled in a very nice fish and gone one step further than my instructions even–he got my knife out and had cleaned the fish. Mike was only about five years old at the time.

Mike and I were duck hunting north of Soda one evening and it was getting pretty cold, so we decided to head for home. We were coming off a hill, when I noticed a huge goose headed straight for us. I told Mike to get down, and as it flew in toward us, I shot it. It was the largest I had ever seen. When I held it out straight away from my body and held it by the neck, its tail feathers touched the ground. It wasn't a Canadian Goose as I thought, but it was an off-white color, so I guessed it to be a snow goose. I took it straight to Wally's to show it off. When he saw it in the car, he said "I don't know what it is, but I know it's illegal." We hustled it into his house and called over his neighbor who was a good friend and an outdoorsman. We found out I had innocently shot a swan! I didn't even know a swan could fly.

Another time, Mike and I went duck hunting with my next-door neighbor who had a large black Labrador dog. As we were getting ready to hide in the brush at the side of a pond, Mike was standing on the edge of the pond and the dog was excitedly racing up and down the shore line. The dog ran into Mike and knocked him into the pond where he got 90% (all but his head) wet. We put Mike in the car and left the heater on while we hunted.

The two best hunts I ever enjoyed were in Soda. One day, Gary Gier and I went down to a pond just off Bear River below Grace. The valley was socked-in with fog that early morning. As we approached the pond, I could hear hundreds of ducks squawking and descending out of the fog through the dark skies to land. When we got to the pond, we wondered whether to put out decoys or just to hide and shoot. We put out the decoys and it took about fifteen or twenty minutes to do so. Ducks were coming in on top of us, trying to land as we were standing in the pond. We both got our limits (seven) in less time than it had taken to put out the decoys.

The best of all hunts was when I had discovered quite by accident where several flocks of geese were spending the day. It was south and slightly east of Soda on a pasture bordering Bear River. We kept an eye on these for about a month before the season began. On opening day, Wally Bennett, Roger Hunter, and I were hidden in a blind, and Gary Gier and Bill Brown were at the other end of the pasture in another blind. We shot fourteen ducks before the geese ever started flying. About nine o'clock, the geese flocks started coming in. They really wanted to land where we thought they would, and we shot thirteen geese in about an hour-and-a-half. Geese are extremely hard to get, so you can imagine the excitement of our success.

Soda had a very good Fourth of July celebration each year. As part of the celebration, about 100 carp were put into a large pool of water in an area of the city park which usually served as an ice skating rink in the winter. Mike was not very effective as a six-year-old, but when he was seven, he waded into the foot of muddy water, caught one, and received a silver dollar for his efforts.

One day, Mike was in the house jumping from the main floor to the family room floor, a distance of five steps down. As he got braver and braver, he jumped from even further back. After a few jumps, we heard a bang and a crack and a yell and a groan and ran to see what had happened. Mike had caught his forehead on the overhang above the staircase and split it open. It took eight stitches. He also cracked his back in the process and had a sprained back for a while. I believe anyone other than a child–whose bones are more pliable– would have broken their back in a similar fall.

In 1975 we moved back to Logan and bought a home being finished at 1633 East 1700 North. This home was very nice, and we were able to get into it because we sold our other home at a $22,000 increase. We sold it for $48,000 to the Kingsfords in Soda. Leonard Kingsford was a lawyer, and his wife had always loved our home. Our home in Logan was extra special to us, automatically, because of large Box Elder trees and a small creek that ran through the back yard. The creek (or ditch) was about fifteen inches deep and offered a cooling effect and peaceful sound in the summertime. We were only a few hundred yards from the mountains, a half-a-mile from church, a mile from the elementary school, two miles from the university, and three miles from town. The new shopping mall and proposed hospital were all being built on the way to our home, so things in the area were very convenient, and the view on the hill very beautiful.

At this point I am thirty-four years old, Mike is nine (which accounts for why he is mentioned so often thus far), Heidi is four, and Shane is nearly two.

Update on Where I've Lived written 2019, age seventy-seven years old

When we divorced, Kay moved to Salt Lake City to an apartment to work for her uncle. I had all four kids in the home on 1700 North. In a divorce you split everything 50/50. I didn't want to give any of my retirement money to Kay, so I arranged to give her the money I needed to from the retirement fund by paying her extra money on the home. Thus she owned about $15,000 to $20,000 more of the house than I did.

Kay told me she was moving back to the house on 1700 North in the spring of 1988. That meant I had to leave and find a new place to live. I decided to live in university housing for convenience. I arranged to live in what was called the Triads, north of Logan Cemetery.

A week or two before I had to move I went to each of my kids individually and told them I loved them, always would, and planned to be involved in their lives. I told them to keep in touch with me as well and I would always be there for them as I'd always be their father.

I figured all the kids would stay with Kay where they could still be in the same home, ward, neighborhood, schools, etc. Additionally, Kay could cook–I couldn't. In fact, I could hardly do anything domestically. Kay was also a better communicator and a warmer personality. She had it all–I had little to nothing to offer the kids. To me it was no decision for them. If I was a kid I'd have stayed at 1700 North. I didn't in any way try to encourage any of them to stay with me.

When I talked to Shane he said, "Dad, I've decided to live with you." You could have knocked me over with a feather. I was shocked. I never asked one child–including Shane–to consider living with me. They all know that. But, I was thrilled with his decision and promised myself to make sure he never regretted making it.

So, Shane and I moved into a Triads apartment (Aggie Village #19D). About a year later Heidi would move to live with her Uncle Owen and her closest cousin Julie. Another two years after that, Mike moved to a home with Sheri in the south part of Logan. Jackie stayed with Kay and Lee at 1700 North.

Shane seemed to really enjoy the adventures of living on campus and he still spent plenty of time with his mother. When in the Triads I kind of reverted to my childhood. Since I was shopping for groceries for the first time I bought lots of pop, ice cream, and junk food. I had one cabinet full of candy and pastry for us to enjoy. I'd buy mostly foods that were pre-prepared. I did try to buy some fruits and vegetables to keep us alive–but only out of a sense of duty.

When Jan and I got married, we moved into her home in North Logan. Kristin was married eight days after us and moved out. Carlo left on his mission to Hawaii the day before Jan and I got married. That left Jan, Kolony, and Carson (Snug), joined with Shane and me. The kids got along beautifully and everyone loved Jan. The big problem was that Kolony resented and probably didn't like me and thus I didn't care for her. I just tried to be pleasant, fair, and honest with Jan's kids.

We did some things to make the home nicer. We took a wood stove from the kitchen area to downstairs. We finished the family/TV room downstairs. We got a hot tub just outside of the family/TV room downstairs. We also built an upstairs and downstairs deck.

After the kids were pretty well gone from the house, Jan felt we either needed to sink tens of thousands of dollars into the house and fix it up, or build another. I wasn't very supportive of either move, but she knew it had to happen. We weren't excited about living on her ½ acre. Way too much yard work.

Jan started looking for lots but not to the point of alarming me. She found a lot that was about $20K-$30K cheaper than the other lots in a development five blocks from where we lived. It was cheaper because of its shape. The shape of the lot would make it difficult to put a home on it. Jan looked at other lots but kept coming back to the cheap one. We now believe the Lord was pushing us in that direction.

Jan finally asked me if I'd put $150,000 toward the lot and a new home. I told her I couldn't as I didn't have that kind of money. I told her I would cash in all my investments and put them on this new project. She agreed to that. Jan got the lot for $40,000 compared to the $75,000 the neighbors paid for theirs.

I'd started investing about age fifty for retirement. My investments came to about $100,000. After tithing a few things I think I was able to contribute somewhere around $60,000 to $75,000. It's been a long time and my figures will probably be off some–but that's my best guess at this time. Jan applied more money than I did toward the new house through her sale of her home that we'd been living in. Thus she had paid for about two-thirds of the home and I paid for about one-third of it. Once in the home I've paid all the mortgage payments on our 30-year loan–which more than evened up the cost.

Jan designed the home and then had an engineer draw up the plans. I left it very much up to her, but there were a few things I insisted on. They were: 1–Stay within the budget. 2–Build it with products that we wouldn't have to paint every few years. 3–It needed air conditioning. 4–An automatic garage door opener. And 5–a tool room.

I got all those things. We've both really enjoyed the home and it would never have happened without Jan pushing everything through to completion. Jan has some great windows so we can enjoy nature while we live there. The home is very functional. We didn't have the money to brick it all-around–but it looks *good from the street. The home must be pretty good as Shane and Kelly Downs have both expressed interest in purchasing it someday. Vic Saunders and my granddaughter Brooklyn both say if they ever build they want to use Jan's plans.*

Prior to this update I failed to mention that I lived six months in army barracks at Fort Ord, California the summer and fall of 1960.

I feel the Lord has had his hand in guiding me to Jan and leading us to our lot on 950 East.

COURTSHIP

The first girl I can ever remember having a crush on was named Linda Nash (I think …). I thought she was pretty cute stuff. This was in about the third or fourth grade. I don't think I even talked to her. She usually stayed with some relative for a few weeks in the summer.

Most of my courting came in the form of wishful thinking. I've never been with a girl who didn't show some interest in me. I guess I was too afraid I'd be turned down or that the person wouldn't enjoy herself. I wasn't very aggressive. Dating, particularly with people I didn't know very well, was very uncomfortable for me, so I seldom dated.

I guess my second girlfriend was a girl in Logan named Carol Schwindiman. I went to a party of hers and then I went on a "kind of" date with her. Several of us boys at Whittier School met several girls at the movie and then we went to the girls' houses and played games.

The closest thing to a real live date was in the seventh grade. I went to a Junior High dance with Joan Stoker (the girl who beat me out in the seventh-grade vice president election). After the dance, we walked downtown to a café and had a hamburger. I remember I had my whole evening ruined because I was worried if I had enough money to pay for the food. I made it by about fifteen cents.

When we moved back to Preston, I went on one or two official dates with Marian Beveridge and Sharon Rawlings, but mostly we'd meet girls at the show or at a high school game. Also, parties were arranged, and the boys and girls were usually matched up, so we'd be with who we liked at the party.

At that age we were all really interested in kissing, and we'd use almost any excuse to get together and kiss the girls we liked. I remember my whole eighth grade year as being full of experiences such as these. Finally, I'd been asked to a girls' day dance with Karen Dunn, who was pretty sharp. I'd met her at the show the week before, and enjoyed her company there. But the Friday of the dance, I got to thinking how dumb all of this activity was, and the more I thought about it, the more disgusted I became.

COURTSHIP

At the end of the class I was in, I found Karen and told her I didn't want to go. When she asked me why, I really couldn't explain the reason. She was pretty upset with me. She was to sing the theme of the dance that night on the floor of the show, and I'd left her stranded. I later heard her mother was really upset with me. It's kind of funny, but from then (eighth grade) until my junior year in high school, I only went on one date, with Marian Beveridge. I felt like I should have a date for the election dance because I was a candidate for student body president of the Junior High School. (I won.)

For those three years of junior high, I did a lot of looking and thinking, but no acting, toward girls. Now that I think of it, I went with Sherlauna Perkins of Smithfield once during my sophomore year. Once again, it was because I had to have a date since all of the other players on our JV basketball team had one. I had met Sherlauna in the neighborhood when she had come up to stay with her cousins. She, as all the rest, was a good-looker. If nothing else, I did have good taste.

During football my junior year, I went with Sherlauna about a dozen times. That's far and away the most I ever dated anyone other than Kay. Sherlauna is a very special person and is very different now than when I dated her. She was rather reserved and shy then, and now she is much more outgoing and personable. I guess that what I'm saying is that her looks appealed to me at that time more than her personality (although she was always very pleasant).

In retrospect, I recall that there were other dates I went on. My only blind date was with a girl named Barbara

Butterworth. I also went out with Julie Hammond, and once had a date with Pattie Telford. Still, all in all, I don't think I went out with more than ten or twelve girls on official dates.

The basketball team went to a party at Christmas-time my junior year. Everyone was to get a date, and we went to Maddox to eat. Dave Keller and I were the only ones without dates. We took a lot of ribbing because we were alone that night. I sat at a table next to Henry Rawlings who had been going with Kay Cherrington for about three years fairly steadily. That night they were having differences over something, and I could tell Henry was upset. Despite this, however, Kay was, as usual, the life of the party. I can remember, earlier that fall, Kay parking in her family's car under our pear trees to the west, and her and Clarene Taylor (my neighbor and her best friend) and Ralph Brenchley (who eventually married Clarene) and me sitting in Kay's old Studebaker eating peas and having a long visit. I guess those two things were a little ground work for what was to come.

Kay and Henry broke up that winter, mainly because Kay wanted to date different people, and when she did, Henry got all upset about it. (I would have, too.) I received a phone call one night in January, and Kay (who had recently moved into our ward) asked me if I would be her partner in the MIA church dancing. I told her I would, and tried to hold down my excitement until she was off the phone. I immediately phoned Scott Tims, a good friend, and told him what had happened. He could hardly believe my luck. He would say things like, "You lucky stiff," "You get all the luck," etc., etc.

COURTSHIP

At this point you need to know that Kay was the most popular girl in the class above us. She was a cheerleader that year, was the junior student body secretary, always held some office or another, was the comedy lead each year in the musicals, etc., etc., etc. Kay later was selected Miss Franklin County right after her senior year and competed in the Miss Idaho Contest, winning one night's competition in talent. Kay was not only good looking, she had a very attention-getting figure, was very talented, and most of all, had a great personality.

We would go to our dance practices and afterward she would drive me home and we would visit for the longest time before she'd go home. We genuinely found each other a lot of fun to be around, and as we grew to know each other (our thoughts, likes, dislikes, etc.), it became a relationship that was pretty comfortable. I guess the only real hang-up I had was that I was afraid what other would think of me going with an older girl who was in the limelight as much as she was.

As we approached the first floorshow that we were to perform (at a church dance), I was wondering how childish it might look to her if I just met her at the dance and had no date. Yet, I was still somewhat afraid of what others would think of me going out with her. Finally, I decided the better of two evils was to ask her to the dance. I think Kay must have made it easy for me, or I'm not sure I'd have had the courage. After that date I think we went out once or twice before I decided I really wanted to start seeing her much more often.

I can remember that not long after our first date, I asked her out for the next Friday, and she said she had a date. So I asked her out for the next evening, for which she also had a date. I think I went through two weekends and she was tied up all the time. The word that she was available had spread rapidly, and she was getting all kinds of offers for dates. I guess I'm not a very good competitor in that type of situation, because I was very unwilling to fight for dates, or to sit and stew about her going out with others while she was dating me. I simply told Kay how I felt at that time, and that if she wanted to go out with me, she could arrange for an evening each week, and if she didn't, she wouldn't.

Kay dated those she had already lined up and didn't accept any more after that. I guess from that point on we went steady, with the exception of a couple of dates she had lined up quite a bit in advance. One was to the BYU Junior Prom and one was with Henry to the High School Junior Prom. (I think she could have gotten out of that one, but when she found out I was going to be away, in New Jersey, she didn't want to miss the dance.) If Kay had continued dating others at that time, I'm sure we'd never have gotten together.

I know it was only a matter of a month or so that I was fully hooked and wishing I were older and in a situation to get married. From that spring on, there was never any doubt about who I wanted to marry. It was probably a good thing (although it seemed like a monumental problem at the time) that Kay would be at USU during my senior year, and that I went to Fort Ord, California for six months the day after my graduation. I'm aware that these circumstances helped us postpone marriage as long as we did.

COURTSHIP

I can remember when I came to the realization that I was really in love. It was when I was in Atlantic City, New Jersey, when I was alone, that I realized I was in love, without any question. Kay had spoken of love a week or so prior to that, and I'd pretty well told her that she shouldn't say something like that unless she meant it, and that I'd never told anyone that and would never do so unless I really meant it. It made her mad enough that she said she wouldn't ever speak of love again unless I felt the same and spoke first.

In 1960, when I came home for a ten-day leave from Fort Ord in July, Kay and I picked out some rings that cost $400, and we got them for $250. I was going to pay for them with my salary from the army. We didn't talk about when I'd give an engagement ring to her, but I gave it to her before I left to return to Fort Ord. Her parents, I'm sure, were not thrilled, and my folks didn't let on about their feelings. However, I think they felt Kay was super, but that I was too young, and they were hopeful that I'd go on a mission first. I'm sure the Cherringtons felt the same way and figured someone older would be much more suited to Kay.

While I was serving my final four months, I got a letter from Kay saying that she'd had an awful lot of people telling her how we were too young and that it was silly to be engaged. She thought it would be best to take the ring off until I got home and then we'd decide what would be the best thing for us. Needless to say, I was crushed. I kept wondering if I was getting the whole story or if there was another guy I didn't know about. I guess I'm like others and always expect the worst to happen. Also during that four months, I got an anonymous letter that basically said, "Too bad, buddy, Kay will never wait." That letter made me mad enough that I wanted to fight the world. Someone was awfully jealous, and I'd have loved to have known who.

I returned from Fort Ord at the end of November and started school for the winter quarter. In January I gave Kay the ring again and we set a date to get married during the Thanksgiving holidays the next fall. We figured we could get through that first year with savings and working part time. Kay would finish her degree at the end of the following summer (she finished college in three years) and could put me through my final two years by teaching.

We were married in the Logan Temple by President Raymond on November 17th, 1961. We went on a honeymoon afterward that included a trip to San Francisco, Salinas (we had Thanksgiving with Aunt Hazel), and back home through Las Vegas. It was a great trip. Dad gave us a new Volkswagen as a wedding present.

We first lived in a basement apartment in Preston for a year-and-a-half. Kay got a teaching job at West Side High School in Dayton in 1962. In 1963 we moved to a nice apartment in Logan at 5th East and 5th North and Kay taught at Logan High as I finished my last year of schooling at USU.

Kay is, and always has been, an immaculate housekeeper. Even if a person looked into a drawer, he would find that she has everything well-organized. She was always taught, "A place for everything, and everything in its place," and she has

COURTSHIP

learned that lesson well. She didn't start marriage as a very experienced cook, but rapidly developed into a fine cook. She was never afraid to experiment and try new things in the kitchen. Kay has always managed our finances. I'm amazed at the number of women who handle family budgets, which makes me feel a little better about our situation. She really does a great job of making ends meet. Kay also does all of the buying (even my clothes). She had done mostly all of the choosing and buying of our homes and has excellent taste.

Kay is a very warm, loving person, and is a great companion. She has more drive (as does most of her family) than 98% of the people on this Earth. She is very industrious. All of the Cherringtons find it difficult to just sit down and do nothing, read a book, watch TV, etc. She has always excelled in all she's done: schoolwork, school activities, teaching, church work, being a mother and wife, etc.

Kay is a creative person and has found it somewhat difficult to be full-time mother and wife at home. I'm sure she looks forward to the day when she can go back to work but will never do so at the expense of the development of our children. She has had several opportunities to teach since our second child (Heidi) but won't think of it until our youngest is enrolled in school.

Kay has served in every church position, it seems, except Relief Society President. She has enjoyed teaching the Gospel Doctrine class and the Relief Society. She has been the Junior Sunday School coordinator, President of the Young Women's organization, and Young Women's advisor. She enjoyed these positions the best. She has served well, but did not at first enjoy being the nursery leader in Relief Society.

Kay does have a fault which is a byproduct of her being so organized and industrious: she has a real problem with keeping her patience. Children, particularly, can annoy her if too many things go wrong. She is aware of this and works at it, but she could still improve there. When she gets that down, she's likely to be "taken up."

If I took the time to write all I know about Kay, I would have written her life history for her, and she needs to do that. Needless to say, I love her and she's a great woman.

Update on Courtship written in 2020, age seventy-seven years old

I've given this section more thought than all of the other sections put together. It will definitely be difficult talking about the divorce and doing my best to be fair to Kay and as honest as I can be. That might be impossible since I see myself as mostly the victim in the whole matter. I'll do my best trying to be as honest as possible.

Being stuck at home with little or no outlet–Kay wasn't very happy with her lot. She admitted to me that she lost her self-esteem and didn't feel her needs were met. She felt unimportant and of little or no worth except to me and the kids.

I suspect this happens to a degree with most stay-at-home moms, but it hit Kay super hard after being so involved in high school and some in college with leadership, drama, music, academics, and kind of being the center of her social world.

I believe she unfairly targeted me and I ended up catching most of her wrath. Not that I didn't deserve some wrath–but not as much as I got.

She kept her growing contempt for me hidden. She never talked to me about how she felt. I think it grew to be an insurmountable mountain when it should never have gotten to that point.

Let me confess to what I see as my shortcomings in the marriage. I needed to be more of a partner in the responsibilities. I could have helped her so much with the kids, food preparation, cleaning the house, laundry, etc.

My mother had done everything for us Hart kids. She found it easier to do it all than to fight us into helping. The same was true of Kay. She did most everything without complaining or pointing out my shortcomings. She kept it all inside where it festered and finally came out in the most negative way possible.

I could tell the last two to three years of our marriage that Kay had changed. Her biggest outlet those last few years turned out to being, first, Ward Young Women's President, and then Stake Young Women's President.

She loved those callings and excelled at them. She received much-deserved praise for her efforts. In fact, when released as Stake Young Women's President she was deeply saddened and somewhat angry. She had found an outlet from being a stay-at-home mom.

COURTSHIP

The last three years I noticed some spiritual changes in her. She stopped saying her prayers regularly before going to bed. She found excuses not to wear her temple garments more often. She started taking little jabs toward the church and had never done that before.

Her relationship with me was changing for the worse. Once in a while she'd say something negative or sharp, like we were enemies rather than husband and wife. Nothing like that had ever happened before. In fact, Kay and I never fought or had critical words toward one another. Most, including me, thought we had the perfect marriage.

I always treated Kay like Dad treated Mother. I had her on a pedestal our whole married life and treated her with great deference. I expect Mark and Reed treated their wives similarly–and it was all due to the example Dad had set with our mother.

On June 2, 1987, just moments before having family prayer and eating dinner, I got a phone call. A drunk woman identified herself and said, "What are you going to do with my husband and your wife?" She went on to convince me they were having an affair.

I knew everyone was waiting on me for our prayer and dinner. I returned to the family and must have looked awful because immediately Kay and Mike asked me, "What is wrong?" I sat there for a moment wondering what to say.

With less than a minute to think about it, I said something very close to this: "Your mother and I love you kids and we're going to do all we can to take care of you, but I've just found out your mother is having an adulterous affair. I'm divorcing your mother because this isn't the first adulterous affair she's had. She's done it before."

With that the kids all started crying, except Jackie. Jackie was only seven and didn't grasp what was going on. Kay left the table without saying anything. She went back to the bedroom and got a couple of things and headed for her car in the garage. On her way past the table where we were sitting, she put a six-page paper titled "The Storm" down in front of me. She left in her car to find her boyfriend, Lee Wheeler, who she thought was fishing somewhere near Preston.

I talked to the kids some more and tried to assure them we'd take good care of them and always be there for them. I told the kids I needed to go talk to their Grandpa Cherrington, the bishop, and Herm Olsen (our lawyer who was a counselor in the bishopric). I informed each of those I visited about what was going on. I also phoned my boss at work, the key guy under me in the office, and my dad.

Getting back to "The Storm": Three years earlier, a huge thunderstorm had passed over Logan. Kay had gone out on the front porch to enjoy the storm and wrote the six pages she gave me when she left the house.

"The Storm" was six pages of how she hated her life, lost her self-esteem, didn't feel anyone cared for her or her opinion, and how determined she was to change her life. I took a real beating in her comments. She blamed me for much of her misery. One of the more significant things she said was, "I'll sell my soul to Satan to change my life." I was in shock at how she felt toward me.

COURTSHIP

Kay had an adulterous affair in the 3rd year of our marriage. It started the summer I graduated from USU. I went to summer school and encouraged Kay to take a swim class because she needed to learn to swim. The instructor was Art Mendini, a PE professor who was most noted for his sports officiating.

Art had a reputation as a "skirt chaser." He had a dark complexion, was enjoyable to be around, and was married with two kids. I selected him as my master's degree professor because I thought he'd be the easiest on me. I had worked with him on the intramural committee the previous two years.

Art went after Kay and Kay was receptive. The affair lasted one to one-and-a-half years and Kay finally told me about it after it was over. Art was only interested in sex and Kay seemed to want more. She finally realized there was no future in the relationship.

It about killed me. I threw up for days. I couldn't eat and all I'd throw up was this bitter bile. I had to know all of the details and they tortured me. When I found out about Lee Wheeler, I didn't seek the details and I handled that much better.

Over time, I came to decide that anyone can make a huge mistake like that, but I couldn't live with or forgive it if it happened a second time. Having decided that, made the decision to divorce Kay so much easier when that time came again.

Over the next several weeks Kay would take off for a few days at a time. She spent some time with Lee, she visited relatives, and she was trying to figure out what she should do with her new life. I had a flare-up of my Crohn's Disease while Kay was in California visiting relatives. I had the kids shipped out to Kay's best friend Jan Curtis's and Kay's dad when I ended up in surgery in the hospital for ten days.

They removed about three feet of my lower bowl that was severely infected and non-functioning due to Crohn's. Someone tracked down Kay in California to tell her I was in the hospital and the kids needed help. She got home the next day to care for the kids while I remained hospitalized.

All the advice I was getting from trusted friends and those in the church was to try to keep the family together. After two to three weeks I told Kay that if she repented, I'd take her back and make the best of a bad situation. Kay's biggest concern if she decided to come back to the family was how I'd treat her. I told her that it would be hard but that I'd do my best. I told her I was only opening that door because of all the advice I was getting and that it wasn't really my personal desire to reunite.

I told her a few weeks later that although I'd opened the door for her to return, that I was going to proceed to work for a divorce, and eventually find another woman to fall in love with and marry. I told her the door to come back would close when I met my new love.

Kay ended up taking a job in Salt Lake City with her uncle who owned a large trucking firm there. She moved into an apartment in Salt Lake City. She worked there for much of the next year and would see the kids on weekends.

My life, like Kay's, had been thrown upside down. I was trying to be a father and a mother for the first time with no experience in cooking, cleaning, shopping, etc. My work had

COURTSHIP

been my full-time job–now I was also trying to manage four kids, in addition to my work. For the next many months my stress level was out-of-sight.

This was a shock to my system, as up until this point in my life, my mother, and then Kay, had taken care of all my needs. I was forced to grow up and take real responsibility for the first time in my life. Real life wasn't fun at all when compared to the life I was used to.

Several things happened during the next many months. Kay dragged her feet on the divorce. I couldn't get her to make decisions on how to split up our possessions. She wanted to keep her options open for the future as long as she could. Finally our divorce became final near the end of October.

Kay talked me into letting Jackie live with Kay's sister Colleen while Kay was in Salt Lake City. Key ended up marrying Lee in April. Shane and I moved into the "Triads" (also known as Aggie Village). This is a married housing complex owned by Utah State University just across the street and north of the Logan Cemetery. Later on, both Shane and Jackie lived there. The only thing special about the "Triads" is its location so close to USU.

Within a few years the divorce had a huge impact on the splitting up of our family. Heidi was living with Owen Cherrington's family. Mike moved in with Sheri south of town. Shane and I lived in the Triads and then North Logan. And Jackie was with Kay and Lee in our home at 1700 North.

After the divorce, I wasn't in any hurry to rush into a second marriage. I simply told my brothers and sisters if they knew of *someone who was attractive, committed to the church, and had a good personality to let me know. I wasn't interested in going to church dances or aggressively seeking someone out on my own.*

A friend and former high school teammate, Pat Hoggan, lined me up with a gal he home-taught named Geri Brown. We double-dated to make it more comfortable. She was attractive and had money she'd gotten from being divorced from her first, wealthy husband. I was thinking this might be from God as Pat had highly recommended me to this gal he'd home-taught for years and she seemingly had a lot going for her.

It turned out she had no interest in me. (I don't think it was personal–she wasn't interested in any guy), and she let me know it rather plainly and quickly. I was a little taken back by it, but I'm glad she did. She was a friend of Jan's and she ended up being a hermit, unhappy, and quite heavy. She made our parting very easy.

Ruth lined me up with a gal that she and Ray knew from the Thiokol Travel Club. Her name was Karen Hunsaker. I dated her for a couple of months. I'd go over and square dance with her once a week, as she had already signed up for the class. We went out to eat and to the movies. I went with her to a Thiokol awards banquet and she came to a couple of Aggie games.

I liked and admired Karen. I think I could have married her and been quite happy. I thought some about it. She had a real good job at Thiokol. She had a small home in Tremonton. I was very unimpressed with her mother, her kids, and her friends. She was the star of her family by far. She was into Western music and dancing and I never have been. I ended up lining

COURTSHIP

her up with my friend Wayne Budge. Wayne and Karen got married and she's been a blessing to him in most every way.

Beverly lined me up with a Hawaiian gal in Bear Lake. I knew as soon as I saw her I wasn't interested. She was a good gal and I enjoyed our date. Her husband dumped her for a younger gal.

During the summer and fall while dating Karen and a couple of others previously mentioned, I had about five different people ask me if I knew Jan King. Then they would say something very nice about her. One was Geri Brown, another was Pat Hoggan, another was a former next-door neighbor, Marietta Sampson, another was a guy, Maurice Thomas who was in the same ward as Jan (and Geri) who worked at USU, and the last one was Sam Morrison, who had the same job I had at the University of Utah and served in the same mission as Jan's former husband.

I'll share with you what Maurice and Sam told me. I did some business with Maurice and when we were done I told him I had some interest in Geri Brown of his ward. Maurice kind of grimaced and said, "She's the most miserable woman I know." He'd had some negative dealings with her about North Logan City. Then he said, "Do you know Jan King?" After I said no, he said, "You should go with her. She's fun, happy, upbeat, and would make any guy extremely happy."

Sam Morrison phoned me a few weeks later, and after conducting our "Placement" business, he asked if I knew Bruce King. I said I knew of him but didn't know him personally. Then I said, "It's funny you bring up his name because I've had several people suggest I go out with his former wife."

Sam enthusiastically said, "I know her and she's terrific. You really should." Sam was the one who finally motivated me to see who this Jan King really was.

I had an organizational Christmas luncheon scheduled in the building just East of Edith Bowen Laboratory School where Jan worked. Three of my kids had gone to elementary school there. I phoned the secretary and asked for Jan's class number. I decided I'd walk through the school slowly and see what she looked like before I decided whether to ask her out or not.

It was recess time when I walked through the school. Jan and another teacher were standing in the doorway to her room visiting as I slowly walked by. Jan asked me if she could help me with anything and I just told them I was going over to the next building. Obviously Jan passed the eye test.

I phoned her that night (about December 20th) and introduced myself and told her I'd had several people tell me I should meet her. I realized she had four kids and Christmas was a few days away, but could she find just enough time to meet and visit over some food.

I think she said she could spare a little time the next evening. We went to Frontier Pies, ate, and visited. I asked her a few questions she wouldn't answer, which turned me off some, but overall, I really liked her and found her to be very personable and fun to be with.

When I took her home I asked her if I could kiss her, even though I realized it was just a first date. She basically hemmed and hawed around and suggested it was too soon. But she was very unconvincing, so I leaned over and kissed her anyway. It

COURTSHIP

was a great kiss and we both reminisce about it to this day. Jan later told me she knew we'd be going out again after that kiss.

I immediately knew I was more smitten with Jan than Karen. Within a week I'd broken off my relationship with Karen. I usually saw in-person or at the very least phoned Jan for something like thirty-eight of the next forty days. By February I knew I was in love with her and told her so. I was equally determined to take my time, look for important characteristics such as a sense of humor, being positive, commitment to the gospel, etc. Instead of just looks and chemistry with the person I considered marrying.

When I met Jan she was almost overwhelmed with responsibilities. She had four kids at home, she had a half-time teaching job, and two other jobs. She was working on her master's degree and then I came into her life and was taking up much of her time. Jan, for the most part, just didn't get much sleep. She'd stay up really late most nights trying to keep her head above water. Somehow, with all that was going on in Jan's life, she started working full-time and finished her master's degree. I don't know how she did it all.

As cute as Jan is, I believe it was her personality that won me over the most. She has a great attitude about everything. She's fun and upbeat and most anyone who knows her is drawn to her. Several friends seek her out for advice and someone to confide in.

Jan is so very different from me in personality. You'd think this would be bad, but it hasn't been. I'm a worrier and she may worry but won't let it dominate her thoughts. I'm a detail person and Jan isn't. I'm very focused on some things while Jan is seldom focused and is easily distracted from what she's doing. Jan is fascinated with everything–I'm not. Living with Jan is a little like trying to herd a cat–it's nearly impossible. Yet I find these differences fascinating rather than distancing. Jan simply won me over in every way.

I could have married Jan most any time after a few months and falling in love with her, but I was very cautious and wanted to take what time I needed to erase any concerns. I was still dealing with many issues at the time. I was feeling my way financially for the first time; I had little experience with money and financial matters. I'd only paid my bills a couple months and had little feel for where I was financially. I needed a newer car badly but didn't know what or if I could afford it. There were many issues like this that made me hesitant to jump into a new relationship.

I also was dealing with emotional wounds. I had gone through serious rejection from Kay. My world, as I knew it, had been turned upside-down. Those types of issues I was dealing with didn't seem very healthy in quickly making new life-changing decisions. I also had a slow-growing feeling of freedom and independence I hadn't experienced after twenty-six years of marriage to Kay. These all added to me taking more time and being more cautious than I normally would have been.

We got engaged at the Glenn Miller dinner dance on campus on February 14, 1989, Valentine's Day. They sold out every night. The guy who played Glenn Miller (Jan Benson) was a work colleague and I arranged a little scenario with him to *ask Jan in front of everyone. He played like he'd found a poem on the floor and read it between dance numbers. I'd written a simple little poem asking Jan to marry me. Then Heidi, who was a waitress at the event, brought out a dozen roses.*

We picked August 3, 1989 to get married. Dad was a sealer in the temple and if healthy enough would perform the marriage. The problem was he was in the hospital at the time of the marriage and one day he was coherent and the next day he wasn't. I'd lined up the temple president to do it if Dad couldn't.

Two nurses with temple recommends volunteered to bring Dad to the temple and assist him. He was attached to an IV tree feeding him what he needed intravenously. It was quite a sight. Dad made one mistake and that was not getting Jan and me to the altar before starting the ceremony. After that, it was perfect. We just had close family there and about a half-dozen close friends. Dad was white as a ghost when done and returned to the hospital. The rest of us gathered at Zanavoo up past 2nd Dam in Logan Canyon for a luncheon.

Before we left on our honeymoon to Lake Tahoe we went to visit Dad thinking it might be possibly the last time we'd see him alive.

Dating for over a year-and-a-half helped us in a few ways. Carlo went on his mission the day before we got married and Kristin married Kelly eight days after Jan and I got married. We heard Carlo was motivated to go on his mission because of Jan's impending marriage to me. It was really good he was gone those first two years, because he had a pretty negative outlook toward me and her marrying again.

With Carlo and Kristin gone, we started out our marriage with Kolony, Shane, and Snug in the house with us. We moved into Jan's house at 2265 North 1250 East in North Logan. We spent approximately fifteen years before we built our new home five blocks southwest of her home in 2005. At that time we had no kids left living with us.

As of this writing, Jan and I have been married for over thirty years. I was married to Kay for twenty-six. Jan and I have had the opportunity to visit many places, many were conferences associated with our work. We've been to Hawaii three times; to all major cities in the west; to Washington DC; New York City; Orlando; New Orleans; Scottsdale; Tucson; and to many resorts in the mountains like Keystone and Aspen in Colorado; Sun Valley, Idaho; and Snowbird and Deer Valley in Utah, etc.

At this time I'm tired of traveling but Jan isn't. She went to Paris with her friend Judy not too long ago. Our big vacation the past fourteen years has been spending January and February in St. George. What a great time to be out of the Cache Valley winter and in St. George where the worst weather that time of year is a light jacket. This is our big event each year.

In a blessing in 1987 my dad blessed me "that the Lord has prepared a woman for you who will be a blessing to you and your children." Jan has certainly fulfilled that. Jan is so fun to live with and share life with. She's funny, optimistic, upbeat, lively, and finds joy in most everything.

Jan's divorce made her a little leery of certain aspects of the church. I've watched Jan grow in her testimony tremendously

COURTSHIP

while being married to her. She has become an all-star at ministering. She has changed lives for the better in her efforts to help out others. She reads her scriptures diligently. She really is doing all she can to make a positive difference in others' lives. Jan has caught up to and passed me spiritually.

I couldn't be happier with the way things have turned out for Jan and me. I believe she feels about me like I do about her. I have no doubt the Lord guided me to Jan to be a blessing to both of us.

EMPLOYMENT

My earliest work experiences were not that early. I don't recall having any set chores or tasks when I was quite young. I do remember helping plan the garden each year which was more fun than work and doing a little hoeing which was more work than fun. We used to help Dad stuff envelopes with advertisements of his books and that was kind of fun. We were always rewarded, it seemed, with a swim at Downata Hot Springs after our work. As I got older, I can remember mother making me scrub the kitchen floor about once every other month.

My first real employment was picking beans. The first time a few friends and I were put on a bus and taken over near

Dayton (five miles west). I was assigned a row and my friends were assigned rows away from me. The beans were really thick and in big clusters and very easy to pick. I felt lost and lonely and started getting sick (all psychological). I hurried down the row just picking the easy clusters and leaving those that were not so readily available. At the end of the row I had become completely psyched out. The owners of the patch phoned my parents and they came after me. Picking beans later became very natural and something we did a great deal of. One of the worst jobs I ever had was thinning beets. With a hand hoe, you'd try to separate the beets so that there would be one every eight to ten inches. You'd be in the middle of a dusty, hot field, bent over or on your knees all the time. It was real bad duty. I had a pretty good job one summer picking apples. The pay was about the same as the other jobs ($4 or $5 a day), but it was fun climbing trees and ladders and eating the product.

My football coach phoned me one day and asked me to pitch peas on his little farm. I was on a truck and when the pea vines dropped in the back of the truck we would spread them around. I worked for a couple of hours before I accidentally stabbed my leg with my fork. Coach took me for a tetanus shot and told me I'd do anything to get out of work.

One summer I poled beans. There were three different tasks with this job: One, poking a hole in the ground with a pointed, metal instrument. Two, placing bean poles in the holes and firming up the hole. And three, tying the tops of the poles together with twine. We started out with twelve guys on

EMPLOYMENT

our crew. After two days they fired all but three of us and got some older or bigger kids. It helped my ego that I wasn't fired.

As I got older I was able to work at California Packing Company which seemed like big money ($1.19 an hour). My first experience at "CalPak" was a bad one. A couple of friends and I got a job at the plant in Smithfield. We worked from 4:00 p.m. to 2:00 a.m. on the worst job in the factory–off-bearing. This is where you crate the canned vegetables as they come off the assembly line. It was a very hot, noisy, and a back-breaking job. I lasted two nights.

My next experience at CalPak in Franklin was much better. I ran a machine that put empty cans on a conveyor belt. When my brother Mark got married I was his best man. This is when I was working night shift on the can machine. I made my own arrangements with Kay's little brother Owen to come down and relieve me for the four hours I'd miss to be the best man at Mark's reception. When I got back from the reception a foreman was there and he chewed me out for taking the time off and not letting him know about it. I felt like I'd really gone out of my way to make arrangements so as not to trouble them and resented the flack I was getting. The foreman then turned to Owen and asked him if he'd like my job. I felt pretty good because Owen was to be my new brother-in-law and I knew he'd look after my interests. Much to my surprise, Owen seriously thought about it. I thought he was sure showing a lack of loyalty to a future member of the family. Owen finally turned it down and I returned to work.

I had another job at CalPak that had a good story related to it. I was driving a forklift which was used to carry pallets of cans around to different areas. One day I decided to drive back of the factory to the cafeteria for a drink of pop. I was traveling at full speed (10-15 miles per hour) when I heard a loud crash and the forklift reared right up in the air as though it was going to rear over backwards. I hurriedly jumped off the machine and got clear of it so I wouldn't get injured. What had happened was I'd left the forklift's front end up at its highest point instead of a few inches off the ground which is the way it is usually driven around. I had to drive between the main factory and the sauerkraut building to get to the cafeteria, and these two buildings were connected by a conveyor belt. The momentum of the vehicle had made it come up on its back wheels with the front wheels two to three feet off the ground. When it happened my gaze was straight ahead and then I was suddenly looking up into the sky at a 45-degree angle. The forklift rolled backwards and returned to its four wheels on the ground with a great deal of noise. I had bent the steel enclosure around the conveyor belt but not done enough damage to cause any harm. I sheepishly got back on the forklift, lowered the fork, and continued my trip. To my knowledge, no one saw this ridiculous incident.

I worked one Christmas holiday season as a clerk in Preston's JCPenney store. I hated being a salesman.

As early as the eighth grade I decided I wanted to coach, so I majored in physical education and picked up minors in driver education and history. Near the end of my senior year I

EMPLOYMENT

had decided to keep going to school and get a master's degree. I was in the process of applying for a graduate assistantship. At the time we had a good friend living in the same apartment house from Malad tell me they had a head basketball position and that I should apply. I said no but he kept encouraging me saying that I could finish my masters in the summers and be picking up some valuable experience in the meantime. Finally I wrote a letter of application and Wayne Budge took it to the superintendent (C.O. Simpson). I got a phone call that day asking Kay and me to come over and interview with the school board the following night. We went over and had the school board and the superintendent interview us both at great length.

Upon arriving home that night we received a call saying we both had jobs if we wanted them. That was the last sleep I had for the next three nights. I lay awake and thought of every conceivable situation that I might run into and how I would handle it. (I'll cover my experiences in coaching in a future section.) I taught Junior High Physical Education and Health, a class of Geography, and one high school class of U.S. History.

I did a very good job of teaching except in my U.S. History class. That was because I went into the class with the idea that I wanted to be a good guy and be popular with the students. I would go in and tell a story or a joke and we'd visit about what was happening around school. They'd talk me out of doing anything, and the class got pretty rowdy with very poor control on my part. The principal had to call me in and tell me there had been complaints from parents and students that they weren't learning anything. I tightened up and things improved but were never as they should have been. The next year I didn't have any problems after Kay coached me a little on what I should do.

I did more in my PE classes than most PE teachers. We combined with the girls and taught social dancing along with gymnastics, tennis, golf, badminton, and many other activities as well as the traditional sports.

In the summers, besides working on my master's degree, I would work for Wayne Budge who was a beekeeper. This was interesting work and Wayne and I became very close as we worked together many times in the wee hours of the morning moving the beehives from one place to another. Yes, I used to get stung once each day even though we wore protective clothing and masks.

Toward the end of my third year at Malad (1967-68) our football coach, Ralph Harding, had to retire. The superintendent asked me if I would handle all of the head coaching duties. I said I would and signed a contract to that effect. I'd just worked for and been awarded double the coaching pay for our district. My first contract at Malad, by the way, was $4,450 for teaching and $650 additional for coaching.

Early that summer the superintendent at Soda Springs had phoned me and asked if I'd come and talk to him about a head basketball coaching position he had. That year Soda had won the state championship and their coach had left for a job as the coach and athletic director at a university in Canada. I

EMPLOYMENT

was quite flattered and decided to talk to them even though I had no intention of leaving Malad and the good teams I had coming up the next three years.

Kay and I went and interviewed with Ellis Williams, the superintendent. He asked us to take the job and really was very complimentary. He made us feel very good toward him and the district. We took jobs because Soda was very modern and progressive in their schools and community compared with Malad. We knew the timing to move could have been better (following a state championship) but felt there would be more future opportunity in Soda. I became the assistant football coach, head basketball coach, and golf coach at the high school. I taught straight U.S. History classes. I also taught drivers education to fourteen-year-olds for the next eight years during the summers and occasionally during the school year.

After the first year, the high school counselor left to be the junior high principal. I told the superintendent that I'd like to be the new counselor, and that I would go back to school in the summer and take night classes in order to certify. He agreed. So from the fall of 1968 through the spring of 1975 I served full-time as the counselor at Soda Springs High School. I really enjoyed that job and finally resigned my coaching, except golf, after my fourth year at Soda. I quit for two reasons: One, I resented the time I was having to devote to my coaching. I guess I was rapidly losing my desire to coach because I started seeing all kinds of other things I wished I could have been doing but couldn't because I had to be at practice or go to a game. And two, we came to a point where we had three straight years of below-average talent and I couldn't see suffering through it. Since I quit I've never missed it at all and have never been sorry.

By the way, after the second year at Malad, I had the principal at Marsh Valley and the superintendent at Grace phone me to ask if I would be interested in coaching at their respective schools. While coaching at Soda Springs, the head coach at Highland in Pocatello, through his brother, informed me that if I'd like to be his assistant, he would see that I got the job.

It looked for a while as if we were going to spend the rest of our lives in Soda Springs, and we were really happy there. I decided that the only thing I'd even look at would be a college position (at one of the colleges between Pocatello and Provo) or perhaps at a counselor position at Preston if it looked like I might eventually take over Dad's home or property or business. So, I was going to be quite choosy.

My freshman basketball coach at USU told me I'd be strongly considered for a job with him in the USU admissions office if it ever opened up, but it never did. When Kay was in labor with Heidi, I went over to ISU Vocational School and filled out an application and talked with the assistant director of the school about counseling possibilities if an opening should occur. Nothing came of it. In March, 1975, a friend from USU, Rod Clark, with whom I worked during my counseling position at Soda Springs, told me of a position at USU that he thought I was quite qualified for. The job was "Teacher Placement Supervisor" at the Career Planning and

EMPLOYMENT

Placement Office. I wrote a letter of application and sent my old, outdated teacher file to the selection committee.

Later that spring while I had a group of students visiting USU, I asked Rod what was happening with the position and he asked me if I'd like to see the credentials of the sixty-nine people who had applied. I looked through the stack of material and stopped worrying about ever getting the position. The sheer number alone looked prohibitive and when I saw that there were a few of them who had PhD's, I wrote the whole idea off.

In June, I got a phone call asking me to come and interview as one of the final candidates for the job. I was highly honored that I had made the final ten or fifteen to be interviewed. I had a group of driver's education kids drive me down as part of our highway driving lesson (I wasn't going to miss a day of work just to interview!). The committee was made up of Rod Clark, Cleone Peterson (who was the outgoing teacher placement supervisor), Eldon Drake (director of student teaching), Al Koch (the newly-hired principal at Preston), and Gil Long (from agricultural education). I think my having a good job and the fact that I didn't think I would have a chance at the position anyway helped me to be relaxed and at ease in the interview. I actually enjoyed the interview very much and must have done quite well.

I got a phone call about a week later asking me to interview with Blair Hale, the director of placement, as one of the three or four finalists. Once again, I went down with my driver's education kids, flattered at how far I had made it, but not really thinking I could get the job. I had a very good interview with Mr. Hale for about an hour and a half, and had a good feeling about it when I was done. That was the first time I seriously started thinking that I might get the job. Mr. Hale told me he'd let me know in about a week what the decision was.

About eight days later, I hadn't heard anything and decided that if I didn't hear by the next day, I would phone their office to see what was happening. My principal told me that he had heard from Mr. Hale and had given him a recommendation for me over the phone. I was also concerned about the salary. The salary was advertised as "negotiable" between $8,500 and $11,500. The year before I had paid income tax on income just short of $14,000. I didn't know if I could afford to take the job if it was offered. I had expressed this concern to those who had interviewed me. During the days between the final interviews, Kay and I had decided that if the job was offered, and if we could afford it, that I should accept it.

On the same day that I had planned a call, Mr. Hale phoned and offered me the job with a salary increase to $12,000. There was no doubt that I should take it, and I accepted the job on the spot. As Kay was listening to me on the phone, however, tears were streaming down her face. She felt as I did that it was the thing to do, but at that point she realized we were going to have to leave the home we had built, many friends, and our close neighbors, the Adams'. I think she was sorriest to leave our next-door neighbors, Dorothy and Evan Adams. I had to finish my driver's education within the next few days and start work the following week. I began work on July 1st, 1975.

EMPLOYMENT

Kay went house-hunting the next week and bought a home that was within two or three weeks of being finished. While I worked the first three weeks, Kay and the kids remained in Soda Springs, sold the home, and prepared to move. I stayed much of the time with Kay's brother Owen and his family. I was given two or three days off to move and we moved to Logan on July 17th.

Update on Employment written in 2019, age seventy-seven years old

I worked six years as an assistant director (we were all called assistant directors) and Supervisor of Teacher Placement. My boss decided to retire. They opened the job of Director up to the three of us assistant directors. There was no question in my mind that I should get the job. Paul Murray was a really good man but highly unorganized and really a "different" kind of guy–not necessarily in a good way. Kathy Adamson frankly had mental problems and little clue as to what happened beyond her "library" responsibilities. She'd already been fired for incompetence from another position at the University before we picked her up.

I decided before any interviews to go to Val Christensen, the

Vice President, and tell him why I should get the job. That didn't go well. He seemed annoyed that I was taking up his valuable time. That really bothered me, but I found out he did that with many of his employees.

I was appointed the Director. I came to find out Blair Hale had already sold Val that I was the person who would do the best job and that it was decided I would be the new director. Blair stayed on one more year as an associate director. We moved to new offices in the University Inn that he'd already designed and spent most of his last year raising funds to furnish. Blair was a great boss and I'll always be grateful to him for what he did for me.

Being the director gave me much more variety in my work and I enjoyed it far more than what I'd previously been doing. I had to set goals, give reports on our work, handle the budget, hire new personnel, and motivate or take care of personnel problems. There was so much more that I'm not including.

I hired the best people I could which always helped make my job easier. I hired a great staff. Generally speaking, my female employees were far superior to my male employees. When I retired after twenty-nine years at USU, I had four women on my staff who could all take my place and do as good or a better job than I did. We had a strong staff.

Besides the raise in salary, and the job being more enjoyable, I got to go to many regional, and a few national, conferences. Expenses were paid by the University and Jan and I got to go to many resorts and destinations that were really fun and exciting. I've been to Hawaii, Orlando, Sedona, Sun Valley,

Update on Employment written in 2019, age seventy-seven years old

I worked six years as an assistant director (we were all called assistant directors) and Supervisor of Teacher Placement. My boss decided to retire. They opened the job of Director up to the three of us assistant directors. There was no question in my mind that I should get the job. Paul Murray was a really good man but highly unorganized and really a "different" kind of guy–not necessarily in a good way. Kathy Adamson frankly had mental problems and little clue as to what happened beyond her "library" responsibilities. She'd already been fired for incompetence from another position at the University before we picked her up.

I decided before any interviews to go to Val Christensen, the

Vice President, and tell him why I should get the job. That didn't go well. He seemed annoyed that I was taking up his valuable time. That really bothered me, but I found out he did that with many of his employees.

I was appointed the Director. I came to find out Blair Hale had already sold Val that I was the person who would do the best job and that it was decided I would be the new director. Blair stayed on one more year as an associate director. We moved to new offices in the University Inn that he'd already designed and spent most of his last year raising funds to furnish. Blair was a great boss and I'll always be grateful to him for what he did for me.

Being the director gave me much more variety in my work and I enjoyed it far more than what I'd previously been doing. I had to set goals, give reports on our work, handle the budget, hire new personnel, and motivate or take care of personnel problems. There was so much more that I'm not including.

I hired the best people I could which always helped make my job easier. I hired a great staff. Generally speaking, my female employees were far superior to my male employees. When I retired after twenty-nine years at USU, I had four women on my staff who could all take my place and do as good or a better job than I did. We had a strong staff.

Besides the raise in salary, and the job being more enjoyable, I got to go to many regional, and a few national, conferences. Expenses were paid by the University and Jan and I got to go to many resorts and destinations that were really fun and exciting. I've been to Hawaii, Orlando, Sedona, Sun Valley,

Vail, Keystone, Aspen, Deer Valley, Park City, Snowbird, Albuquerque, Tucson, Phoenix, San Diego, Las Vegas, Los Angeles, San Francisco, Seattle, Portland, Lake Tahoe, Reno, and others. The twenty-nine years I spent at USU were really great. Being the director I made almost twice what my assistant directors made. This also sweetened my retirement.

I was going to retire after thirty years. I found out I wasn't gaining anything financially to go to thirty so I ended up retiring after twenty-nine years at USU and eleven years as a teacher, coach, and counselor at Malad and then Soda Springs.

Retirement is the best. Every day is Saturday in that you can decide to do what you want. Between Social Security and the State of Utah retirement, we have enough money to do most of the things we'd like to do. We aren't well off, but there are lots of people we wouldn't want to trade places with. Jan's in a similar situation as me.

FAMILY

My mother's family has always been a bit of a mystery to me. She was born and raised in Lethbridge, Alberta, Canada, and the members of her family have never lived close to us. Neither they, nor we, have traveled great distances to visit and we have all seldom seen one another. Mother told me that her father died of appendicitis and that her brother died of Bright's disease. I'm not certain of the age of either of them when that happened.

There are two people I knew better than the rest: one of these is her mother (Grandmother Towell), who, at this time, is still living. She has visited us about once a year. When I was very young, perhaps four to six years old, our family went to Lethbridge and spent a week. Grandmother remarried–a man by the name of Percy Towell, who died a very few years ago. The other person I got to know well was Mother's sister, Hazel Towne. Hazel and her husband, Wesley, live in Salinas, California, and I've eaten two Thanksgiving dinners there. I also spent several weekends there while I was in the Army. They're both great people. They have two adopted sons, Jeff and Craig. Mother's other two sisters, Dora and Bea, live in British Columbia and Alberta, respectively. I don't know that I've seen either one over three times in my life, which is really too bad, as I'd like to know them better.

My dad's family live mostly within a 100-mile radius of the Cache Valley area. Dad's father, Arthur William Hart, had two wives, Grandmother Ada Hart and Aunt Vadi. I can barely remember Granddad. He died when I was five or six and I can remember his funeral. Grandmother Ada Hart died four or five years ago. Aunt Vadi is close to ninety years old and still living. Between the two women there were twenty-one children (two died early or the number would have been twenty-three). The oldest was Uncle Arthur who died of a heart attack around age fifty-eight. He smoked and ran a music store in Preston. He and Belva had two boys and a girl.

Uncle Halo was next. He is now retired from the Post Office where he was Postmaster. He and his wife Margie had one boy and four girls. They got a divorce when the youngest child was grown. Marge was about twenty years younger than Halo and wanted to make a life of her own. Both are still active in the church but have not received a temple divorce.

Dad was third. From here on, I'm not sure of the ages of the children, but I'll list them in the order that I think they were.

Aunt Evadna married Elmer Lawrence and had two boys and two girls. He worked for the fire department in Logan for many years.

Adena Wixom raised two boys and a girl. Her husband died of a heart attack in his fifties. Their boy, Doug, was my closest cousin and was the only one with whom I ever stayed or that ever stayed with me. They lived in Salt Lake City.

Elna Palmer raised a bunch of boys and also lived in Salt Lake City.

Uncle Reed was always a favorite of mine. Dad had told me about what a great track man he was (mile and cross country) and I always looked up to him. He and Letha raised two adopted girls in Salt Lake City.

Wendell raised a small family in Salt Lake City and Grand Junction, Colorado.

Joel has been in Salt Lake City and also raised a small family. Joel, I later found out, is a lawyer, but never practices.

Aunt Arlette Day runs Murray Music and is really a bubbly personality. She and her husband have four or five children.

Uncle Brett married a real beauty. I always though Rene was just like a movie star.

Neal and his wife raised five good-looking boys and one girl in Salt Lake City.

Ada Shumway raised a small family in Shelley, Idaho.

Jocelyn was the youngest child and married Frank Fox.

One Aunt named Hermoine lives with Aunt Vadi. I don't

know her story but have understood her to be mentally retarded.

My uncles Newell and Newt were kind of "black sheep," as far as the church goes. Newell left Preston and went to San Francisco for several years. He grew his hair out long and lived a hippy-type existence. He came back to Preston a few years ago and made his home from a tavern on the west of town. He is extremely talented and has written a lot of historical articles and books. Though he has little direction in his life, he really is a good man.

Newt was always very rowdy. He was a rodeo man, usually bulldogging, and I don't think he's ever held down much in regard to permanent work. The last I heard of him, he was tending bar in Salmon, Idaho. He was a good-looking man.

Rhea married Wallace Grandy and raised a small family in Smithfield, Utah.

Jed raised a small family in Salt Lake City and works at Kennecott Copper Corporation.

Sabrina married Ulyss Nash and lives in Preston, Idaho.

Uncle Mickey is perhaps the most creative and talented of them all. He is the moving force behind a chain of Hart Brothers music stores in Utah and Idaho. Most of my uncles have worked in these stores and most are musically inclined. Everyone likes Mick. He has written and published a great many church songs and also wrote a musical that hasn't "made it" as yet.

I really admire most of my uncles and aunts and feel they are outstanding people. I have become well acquainted with most of the people (and there are very many, as you see) in

FAMILY

my dad's family through the family reunions they have each year. I knew most of my cousins, though I did not feel much kinship with most of them as I have had little interaction with them other than the reunions.

I would really like to talk about each member of my own family but because of time and space, I will only touch on the basic personalities and talents of each.

Dad (Marcus) is extremely talented. He is gifted at writing and has made his living the past twenty-two years from a vocabulary book he compiled. He has written his autobiography (part of it) in a book called "Apple Blossom Daze." It has never made a great deal of money, but it is well-read in the Cache Valley area and is very entertaining. Dad has published a book of poems, also. He has written many articles and poems which have been published in church and other magazines. Dad is also musical and plays the violin and has learned to play the piano on his own during the last few years.

Dad has a meek personality in some ways. His kindness in unexcelled. He has always set a great example and has taught his family "the Lord's way." He's never really felt that his talents have been fully known by others, is very proud of his accomplishments, and I think sometimes feels that his accomplishments go unnoticed. They surely aren't unnoticed by those of us who know him well, though. He's been a temple officiator for about thirty years and is presently a sealer. He has married the last three or four children in our family in the temple. He is presently serving as the executive secretary of the Preston South Stake and is doing a very outstanding job. He loves to go on hikes and usually goes for about an hour and half each day down along the Bear River where he played as a kid.

Mother (Clara) has really been a selfless "slave" all of her life, devoting most of her energy to her children. Mother quit school when she was early in high school to work and help to support the family. When her dad died she did ladies' hair, etc. She feels uneducated, but through her continued reading she is probably as educated as, or more so than, most people. While raising her nine children, she has never worked outside the home and has always been there to help her children. I'll bet in her lifetime she has done the work of five or six modern-day wives and mothers. Mother is now enjoying her leisure after all her children have left. She is always reading a good church book or doing something interesting. Mother has always been very healthy and kept herself very attractive. At age sixty-seven she could easily pass for fifty. Almost every time I've introduced her to someone, they have commented on how nice-looking she is. I don't know how mother has done it, but she hardly ever complains and yet never had much of a change of pace from her duties at home.

JoAnn was an excellent student. She had a great deal of creativity in her that she hasn't had the opportunity to give full outlet to. She is seven years older than me and is married to Perry Roberts, an ear-nose-throat specialist. She has five boys and two girls who are also all very creative and outstanding. She was the valedictorian at Logan High School, but as she did not move there until her senior year, she let the other person who was next in line have the honor since they had lived in Logan all their life.

Mark is four years older than me and many of the things that I tried to do were because Mark had done them. He has always been a lot of fun to be around and is kind of a live-wire, always trying to get something going. He married Joan Geddes, who was a year behind me in school. They have four boys and three girls. Mark is a great promoter. I think he is highly motivated by money. After teaching a year of seminary, he has been in various areas of selling. He changes jobs about as often as I now see him, which seems to be yearly. He seems to better himself with each move and at present is doing better than he ever has before. He and JoAnn both are now living in Missouri. Some of the family members joke that when Dad dies, Mark will finally have a steady job (most feel that Mark will be inclined toward taking over the family business). This is said in a joking manner and is not meant to be demeaning in any way.

Carolyn is also a real live-wire. She is two years younger than me and is always doing something creative. She teaches school and really gets into things like directing an assembly, musical, or dance concert. Around home she loves to do macramé or knit or anything except the menial housewife duties. She married Wally Bennett, who teaches band at Soda Springs at present. Wally is something else. I could spend several pages telling stories about Wally, but I won't. Most would be very interesting to read, but perhaps also could be embarrassing. Wally is both a real character and a great guy.

We did an awful lot together when we were both in Soda; I really enjoyed his association and friendship. They now have three boys. When I was young and growing up, I remember giving Carolyn a rough time and putting her down many times, but I now really think the world of her.

Beverly is also a very creative person who has been frustrated and stifled somewhat. She married early and had children all born close together. She married James Robinson of Preston and now lives in Georgetown, Idaho. James works at Monsanto in Soda Springs. Beverly is the most musical in the family. She took piano lessons from Professor Wasserman at USU for several years and plays well. She sings, as do each of the girls in the family, and was a very good student. I identified with Beverly a great deal when I was young. She is very family-oriented and calls various family members often. She likes to have family get-togethers.

Bonnie is the most reserved of all the girls, if not all of the family. She sometimes displays a lack of self-confidence, though she is very capable and talented. Bonnie is very idealistic and in that respect is like her mother. She displays more femininity than some of the others, and is a very concerned and dedicated mother and wife. She married John Murray of West Point, Utah, and they have three children. They plan to move to Denver this summer, after having been in New York City for some time. They are looking forward to being in the west and closer to home and family.

Shelley looks most like her mother. She is a very good singer and spent one summer in West Yellowstone performing in a theater group from Ricks College. She met her husband at Ricks (he played football there). They live on a farm in Moore, Idaho (close to Arco) and have four boys. She has the only set of twins I know of in the family. Shelley is very content and happy and expresses this to others. She enjoys her role as a wife and mother and also loves the family get-togethers.

Ruth is very much like Carolyn in her personality–very outgoing and forward. Ruth is a real ham and loves to perform. She sings very well. She is the only child who has attended Snow College and Weber State. She married Ray Huff, whom she had never met when he told her he wanted her to be his wife. At the time, Ruth was writing to Ray's companion, whom she had known at school. Then she and Ray began to correspond and their relationship grew. Ray is now continuing his education and they are expecting a baby in the fall. Ruth has been working at a bank in Brigham City, where they are living at present.

Reed is in the beginning months of his mission in Louisiana. Reed is an extremely nice-looking young man, and has a very pleasant personality. Probably his greatest loves are hunting and fishing, which he spends a great deal of time at. Reed is a natural athlete but did not participate much in school because he was late in developing this interest. Reed is the only member of the family with mechanical abilities and excels in auto mechanics and welding. He had a bit of a struggle going through school because he was late in developing an interest in academics, though he was very capable. About a year prior to his mission call he struggled quite a bit with some of the Word of Wisdom. Everyone in the family was very concerned, but Mother and Dad worked very closely with him and he eventually worked out the problems he had. Prior to his mission he read many, many church books and the scriptures. He is very well-read. He is a very great kid and we're all proud of him.

Kay's family is very similar to mine in some respects, and very different in others. They have the same church background and the same environmental background (father a teacher, mother in health foods, living in Preston) but they were raised much more rigidly and are much more productive than our family. Kay's family members are "workaholics." They push themselves to the limits and have a hard time letting down and relaxing or enjoying leisure time.

Kay's father, Jack Cherrington, taught seminary most of his life. He was an outstanding athlete at USU and majored in agriculture. He is a very wise and gracious person.

Kay's mother, Virginia Freebairn, was a most warm and loving person. She was completely dedicated to her family. She graduated from the University of Utah. She was a very good violinist. She had cancer and died in 1968. She was very ill and struggled with her health off-and-on for fifteen or twenty years before she died.

Kay's step-mother, June Sorenson, is a native of Logan and has been good for Mr. Cherrington. They both seem to be enjoying their years together.

Kay, the oldest of the family, was actually the mother of the household much of the time because of her mother's sickness.

FAMILY

The members of her family hold her in special regard like no other brother or sister relationship I've ever seen.

David is my age. He was a very good athlete. He lettered in college in track (hurdling and high jump) and was very good in high school football. David got his PhD in Organizational Behavior and is rapidly becoming one of the top men in his field in all of the U.S. He is highly motivated and loves his work. He and his wife Marilyn have two boys and two girls and live in Orem. David teaches at BYU; he is highly motivated by notoriety and productivity.

Owen is two years younger than me. He got his PhD in Accounting and is a CPA. Owen, like David, is also excelling in his field. He and David are both continually involved in writing textbooks and doing research work in addition to their teaching assignments. Owen also has a large consulting business on the side. Owen is highly motivated by money. Owen was also a good high school athlete in basketball and track. He and his wife, Kris, now have three girls and live in Logan where he teaches at USU.

Coleen is four years younger than Owen. She is a very selfless and giving person. I think she has suffered (at least I think that she thinks she has) from being in Kay's shadow. She has a great deal of talent and ability. She got her degree from BYU, as did David and Owen. Her first husband, Max, was killed in a car accident when their son was nearly one year old. She is now married to Mike Smith and they have one child. Max was a policeman. Mike is finishing his education at the present in the field of special education. They live in

Clearfield. Coleen has taught school (usually the 1st grade) for many years in Kaysville and Clearfield.

Joe, the youngest, has just finished his degree in music at BYU. Joe is able to relax and enjoy himself better than the others and is less driven. Joe married Debbie Cahoon last winter in Cardston, Alberta, Canada (Debbie's home). He has been very active in the music and drama department at BYU and has participated in the music and drama department at BYU. He has participated in many musicals and operas. His singing talent is well-known. In addition to the operas and musicals, he has been known for his singing of the "Star Spangled Banner" at all the BYU home basketball games the past year.

Coleen and Owen, I feel, follow the physical attributes of their father, while Kay, David, and Joe seem to resemble the features of their mother's family more. I really enjoy each of Kay's brothers and sister and their spouses. I have great admiration, respect, and friendship with all my in-laws.

Both my own family and in-law family are very family-oriented and try to get together often. Consequently the children know all their cousins on both sides very well and Kay and I are able to see and associate with brothers and sisters and their families relatively often. These family get-togethers are big events and highlights in our lives.

Update on Family written in 2019, age seventy-seven years old

Here is more from the last approximately forty years about our family. I'll start with my kids.

Mike is now about fifty-two. He was quite popular in high school as a comedian. He married Sheri Dubach from Kaysville and they have two boys, Shawn and Dillan. Sheri's dad and brother have been into drag racing most of their lives and Mike got his boys into it. It has been the family thing to do and both boys have had many successes.

Mike is a hard worker. He has worked in the prison supply business most of his life. He's been quite successful.

Shawn works at an auto body shop and still is into drag racing. Dillan is probably done with the racing. He graduated from high school this spring and enters Weber State for engineering as a junior in a few weeks.

Sheri has worked as an aide in schools in the Layton area.

Heidi graduated in business from BYU. She married Jeff Lewis from Tooele. Jeff graduated from Utah Valley University in Orem. Jeff has made a good living in the delivery business. Jeff is about to be released as bishop of his ward. Heidi has been the manager of H&R Block in Tooele recently. She has been a shoe store manager. She has been a stay-at-home mom while raising her kids. They live in Tooele. They have three girls and a boy.

Tori is in her early twenties. She's a lovely girl who loves children, her family, and her friends. She's our oldest grandchild.

Brooklyn was a volleyball player at Tooele High School. She went to BYU-Hawaii and married a returned missionary from Mesa, Arizona who she met there. Odds are she'll have our first great-grandchild.

Aysha is going into her junior year this fall. She is a student athlete. She will start varsity in volleyball and was MVP of the team as a sophomore in basketball last year. She's also been on the golf and track teams.

Crew is a budding athlete for Tooele. I think he starts high school the year after next. He's a real speedster which helps him in all sports.

Shane went to Western Wyoming Community College after high school, where he played basketball the year before his mission and the year following his mission. He met his first wife, Katie Rehrer from Pocatello, there. Shane had a nice basketball career at Logan High School. He was on the varsity three years, a *starter on the varsity two years, and leading scorer his senior year.*

Shane finished his bachelor's degree at Utah State University. His first job was in Seattle. He got laid off, and then got a job in Thousand Oaks, California. He decided to pursue an MBA and went to the University of Chicago which turned out to be the #1 rated MBA school in the world that year. His first two jobs after graduating he lost in massive layoffs. He worked in Louisville and Augusta. He took work with the FAA in Washington DC and has been there ever since.

Shane and Katie had Colin, a very good athlete and a sophomore this year in Virginia; Spencer, a happy kid who has some promise in sports; and Mollee, a 3rd grader and a real cutie.

Katie went off the deep-end and divorced Shane. Shane was devastated. After a couple of years, friends talked him into joining a dating service. Though hesitant, he soon made contact with the one the Lord had prepared for him. They quickly fell in love and are now married with a young daughter named Sophia.

Sophia looks a lot like Chris with her dark hair and dark eyes. Everyone thinks their grandkids are very bright, but Sophia is extremely bright. She has a vocabulary much more like an adult than a child. I predict Sophia will excel in school and at creative activities. Sophia has a very warm and loving personality. Shane has shared many humorous stories about how Sophia thinks and reacts to certain situations.

Shane's wife Chris is a very successful banker who has two older children in college. Mary is the oldest. She served a mission on temple square. John is still living at home and going to school. Chris has been a real blessing to Shane.

Jackie was recognized for showing the most spirit and personality at Logan High School. She married a good friend and classmate from LHS, Jeff VanZanten. They have two boys, Ty being the oldest. I think he's about a 9th grader this fall. Ben is in about the 4th grade. Both boys are successful and doing well. They live in Jackson, Wyoming.

Jackie graduated from USU with a master's degree in Speech Pathology. She worked for Cache School District before moving to Jackson.

Jackie and Jeff got divorced and Jeff eventually remarried. Jackie is really involved with an improv group that performs in Jackson from about October to May. She's very close to those in the group and they are her best friends and her support system. Jackie works full time as an audiologist for the schools there. She had to get more training in audiology to gain an endorsement to work in that area.

Moving on to my siblings now ...

JoAnn died at about age eighty-three. She spent her last few years in a nursing home in Preston. She had Type-2 diabetes.

Mark lost his wife Joan. She had Parkinson's Disease. Mark remarried a former friend of Joan's and his from when they lived in the Seattle area. Her name is Kaylene. They seem to be enjoying their activities with one another. Mark's big hobby is fishing. He goes about once a week on the upper Provo River in Heber Valley. He has pretty good success.

Carolyn and Wally have lived twenty miles south of Rexburg for years. Carolyn wrote two books. The first was about saints' travel by ship to the U.S. The second traces their travel from the east coast to the Omaha area. She is trying to get them made into movies. The Bennetts have come to St. George with us the past few years. We've had a great time visiting, going to movies and shows, golfing, playing pickleball together, etc.

Beverly and James got married and divorced twice. She was a Postmaster in St. Charles and Weston. She lived in Preston for many years. This year she just moved to Boise and lives with Rachel, her husband, and their two boys. We will miss her being close by. More than anyone else she has been the glue to the family–organizing family gatherings and keeping us all in touch.

Bonnie and John raised a nice family. Most live in the Denver geographical area. Bonnie has gained some notoriety for writing the words to several LDS church hymns written by Janice Kapp Perry. She will probably go down as the most notable of Mark and Clara's children.

Shelley married Seth Beal whom she met at Ricks College (now BYU Idaho). After Ricks they took over his dad's farm outside of Arco, Idaho at a place called Moore. They raised a large, successful family. Seth served as a county commissioner for two to three decades, was a bishop of their ward, and then served as Stake President. They are now finishing up an assignment in the Idaho Falls temple presidency. Both are very impressive, down-to-earth people.

Ruth married Ray Huff of Brigham City. Ruth and all my sisters are all outstanding singers and Beverly is an outstanding pianist and organist. Ruth had two boys and adopted a boy and a girl who both had a lot of issues. Ray served as bishop in two different wards. They lived in Brigham and later moved to

Perry. I believe they're very happy and successful at this point in their lives.

Reed married Susan Rallison from Franklin and they live in the house at 161 South and 3rd East in Preston where we grew up as kids. Reed and Susan raised five kids. Their youngest was a good basketball player for Preston High.

In Kay's family, Kay and Lee Wheeler live in St. George. Kay has had many physical challenges in the past three decades. I understand she's replaced both hips, both knees, both shoulders, and had a narrowing of her spine injury.

Kay's dad and step-mother (June) have been on the other side for a while. Her brother Owen died in his sixties from a brain tumor. Owen was blessed that he would be given time to organize his affairs and that was fulfilled. I think he had about two years to do that.

Coleen and Mike have both retired and now live somewhere in or near Huntsville. Coleen was in charge of all of Davis County's elementary education program. Mike was a professor in Education at Weber State University.

David finally retired at about seventy. He always loved his work. They served a mission back in New Jersey where Marilyn was raised and David served his mission.

Joe retired from being a teacher, then an administrator, in Sugar-Salem schools. He's currently serving a mission in Tennessee. They raised a large family.

After being divorced from Kay, I've had very limited information about their family and even less contact. I've always had great admiration for their family and they've all been great to me. The Cherrington's are one of the outstanding families in the church. They deserve the best.

Here's a rundown on Jan's children: Kristin married Kelly Downs from Smithfield after his mission. They were married a week or so after Jan and I got married. They have lived in Logan (at the USU trailer court), Providence, and Syracuse, Utah. They have three children: Kellstin, often called Beans, Kristelle, often called Krissy, and Klansy, often called Belle. Each name is derived from a combination of Kelly's and Kristin's two names. Kristin is presently teaching kindergarten in the Davis School District.

Kellstin is nearing graduation from USU. Klansy starts her sophomore year at USU this year and Krissy has been attending SUU in Cedar. They're all great kids.

Carlo lives in Salt Lake City. He earns money doing a few things like tinting windows or driving a bicycle taxi. He enjoys reading and time with his dogs.

Kolony graduated from USU and worked in her field (interior design) before marrying Brett Tippetts from Kaysville. Brett has been very successful in advertising and now is a partner in their own new advertising firm in Salt Lake City.

Kolony worked with a local company designing products for young mothers that was very successful and sold nationwide. When the company was sold for $20-$40 million she quit work and they've been raising a family of three.

Kapri is in high school and very artistic. Kohler is twelve and knows technology that is amazing. He's very bright. Klover is seven and starting second grade.

Carson (who everyone calls Snug) has chased his kayaking

passion and love for the outdoors to Asia, Costa Rica, Mexico, and all over the western U.S. He settled in the Jackson, Wyoming area by design. He used to work to have enough to chase his passions. He married Erin Munk of Benson and they have two girls. Harper is in the middle of elementary school and Revyn goes to first grade this year. These girls are following Snug's interest in outdoor adventure.

Snug got a job at Jackson High School teaching immersion Spanish. He worked hard to go back to school and become qualified. They bought a terrific home in Alpine, Wyoming with an amazing yard. You'd have to say Snug seems to be living the dream right now.

THE PRESTON HIGH SCHOOL INDIANS, nearing the crest of athletic performance this year, pose here in anticipation of Wednesday's game with Pocatello High School at Pocatello and a tilt with BY High School at BYU fieldhouse Saturday night. The five seniors and eight juniors on the Indian squad have four wins to their credit this season. They have lost two games. The team started good this season and has been able to maintain their winning streak quite well. The team starts fifth district league play Jan. 9 with Malad in the PHS gymnasium. Squad members are, left to right, front row, Robert Hawkes, manager; Coach Ivan Davis and Edward Burrup, manager; back row, left to right, Dean Checketts, Jeff Hyde, Trent Packer, Steven Porter, Malin Davis, David Hart, Rodney Larson, Wallace Bennett, Lorenzo Griffeth, Pat Hoggan, Dee Ward, and Verl Christensen. Reid Carlson was absent when the picture was taken.

ATHLETICS

The first competition in which I remember participating was playing marbles. In the third grade, Orval McKenzie and I used to go over to the middle school (Jefferson) and win marbles away from kids two and three years older than we were. We both were really very good and wound up with a tremendous collection of marbles. A few years later, Orval won the Logan City marble championship in the sixth grade. He and I were about equal in ability.

    I remember having footraces in the fifth grade with other kids in my class. I finished second to Lorenzo Griffeth. From that point on, either I got slower or my classmates got faster, because I was later very average in speed.

When I moved to Logan in the fifth grade, all the kids were playing touch football during recess. I found that I had good abilities for catching a ball. I'm sure this helped my being accepted as well as I was, because I immediately became an important part of the team. Therefore the team and the sport also became important to me.

In the sixth grade I participated in a junior pentathlon sponsored by the Deseret News. Each boy in each school participated in about eight or ten events and received an awarded number of points for his accomplishments in each event. I finished third in the sixth grade in spite of the fact that I was only average in my running, jumping, and throwing events. I really excelled in one event, though: A person would see how many basketball shots he could make in a two-minute period of time, shooting from outside a semi-circle about eight-to-ten feet away from the basket. I remember that I made thirty-two baskets, substantially more than anyone else. I made enough excess points in this event to win a certificate and compete on the next highest level.

Each elementary school in Logan had a Little League baseball team, and both my fifth and sixth grade teams finished second in a league of six teams. In the sixth grade, an all-star team was selected from among the six teams. Usually one or two players were chosen from each team and the all-star team chosen was able to play Tremonton and Ogden. I was very excited when I made the team and started at second base.

From these and other experiences, I found that I could be creative and get recognition from participating in sports; and

ATHLETICS

most any sport that involved a ball came quite naturally to me. I guess by the sixth grade, I had become a genuine "sports man." I knew every Major League baseball player, his batting average, number of home runs, etc. At that time, baseball was my sport, and I spent all my time involved in it. Duke Snider of the Brooklyn Dodgers was my hero, and the Dodgers were my favorite team. I was an avid Yankee hater. In those days they were winning all the World Series'.

In the seventh grade in Logan Junior High, the PE instructor (Lincoln McClellan, now at USU) had a super PE program and intramural program. He used to have skill tests and gave so many points for doing certain levels of accomplishments. They had a "500 Club" with names of students who had achieved 500 points in each of the ten to fifteen tests of skill during the year. I had a goal of reaching the "500 Club" and made it through more than half of the tests when I finally fell short at push-ups. I couldn't do them. I remember also that to make 500 points in free-throws, one had to make five out of ten. There were only two or three of us who made it.

When I moved back to Preston in April, I found everyone talking about basketball and what a big deal it was in Preston. I was kind of upset, because baseball was my favorite sport and I found that Preston's summer program wasn't up to much.

In the eighth grade there was no football team or baseball team, only a basketball team. No wonder they really liked basketball. I made the eighth grade team and was a starting guard. We played Whitney, a very big and good team; Franklin, a generally poor team; and West Side, a pretty good team. We were so much bigger in population than the rest of them, and yet the only team we beat was Franklin.

I remember I scored three points in my first game. I thought that was pretty good. My biggest game that year was in a tournament. I scored the first seven points of the game against Whitney, all in the first quarter. We beat them for the first time, but I didn't score any more points during the game. Coach Amos appreciated my interest and knowledge of sports. He used to call me into his office and ask my opinion of whom I would start, etc. It was about this time that I decided I wanted to coach. I'm sure he whetted my appetite by involving me in what he was doing.

During the ninth grade, we got to play football for the first time. We didn't do very well. I remember Dan Palmer, our fullback, was very mature at that age and used to drag tacklers with him. I played quarterback and I used to call any two plays and then on the 3rd play I'd give it to Dan, knowing he'd get us a first down. I enjoyed calling plays, running, and passing, but I hated to play defense. Every time I ever tried to tackle someone, I'd get hurt, and I didn't like that. That was true of my whole experience in football.

Also during the ninth grade we played about a fifteen game basketball schedule. I played guard all through school because some of the guys got taller at a younger age than I did. I kept growing and moved from being slightly bigger than average size to being bigger than all of them in height during my junior year. My junior and senior years brought with them an attempt by the coaches to switch me to forward or center; but I was a guard, I thought, and would sulk and not do as well. So, they'd move me back before long and let me play guard, although they did make me play underneath on defense because of my height.

It was quite a thrill for me to play Logan and play against all my old friends. The first game at Preston, I scored ten points and did very well. The second game in Logan (where the girls could see), I scored only two. I averaged about six points a game that year. My best game was against South Cache. They were playing a zone defense and we were having trouble getting inside of it. I made seven long shots for fourteen points.

My sophomore year in high school found me playing on both the sophomore and the junior varsity football teams as quarterback. We had a pretty good year and I was the leading scorer with three touchdowns. I can remember the weather that fall was very nasty, and I hated to practice because it seemed all we did was hold dummies for the varsity to practice against. I held the safety dummy and the weak side of the line would brush block, run about twelve yards, and throw flying cross-body blocks on my dummy. My hands would be cold and would seem to almost break off when the dummies were hit. I guess it was part of my initiation. The seniors would really show off and give it to us sophomores in every drill they could.

In basketball in the tenth grade I was the main starting guard on the junior varsity team. We were a so-so team until the end of the year when we won six of our last seven games. I averaged around seven points a game and was turning into a pretty good passer at this time. My best game was a fifteen point effort against Montpelier. Our coach, Vic Jensen, would sometimes pick the starters by the first five to shoot around the court at five spots about twenty feet out. Since I was one of the two best long shots on the team, I never had any trouble starting. The problem was that usually we'd start three guards, and our center, who couldn't shoot outside, would have to come in off the bench.

Jensen wasn't the best coach in the world. Right at the first of the year he had ten juniors and ten sophomores on the team, and I was getting so little playing time in the first two games that I and one of the juniors were planning to quit. I had decided that, during one game, if this person had gotten up and walked off the court, I was going to go with him right during the game. We didn't, however, and shortly after that, Jensen cut the team and I found myself playing most of the time. I remember one game against Marsh Valley. There were two seconds left in the first half, and I threw a running two-hand shot from the middle of the backcourt and it banked in right at the buzzer. Steve Porter and I were invited to practice with the varsity during the Thanksgiving holidays and we thought that was pretty big stuff. But we were still too undeveloped to stick with them.

Our coaches used to require that we go out for track each spring if we wanted to play football that next fall. I didn't have track talent and preferred baseball, so I always quit after two or three weeks, knowing that the coaches wouldn't really keep me off the team. I played baseball that year, but I only got

ATHLETICS

into one game. I did get an infield hit, however, in my only appearance at bat. I also remember I played in one varsity football game for a couple of minutes that year when we were way ahead of one team.

We had a very good football team during my junior year. We had a senior quarterback, Dave Keller, who was very good. For experience, the coaches had me play on the junior varsity team. I also played on the varsity when we were far ahead or when the coach wanted a special play sent in. The junior varsity was especially fun, as we played against kids who were either younger than us, or were the same age, but they were never older. We played Marsh Valley in McCammon one afternoon. I received the second half kickoff. I ran straight ahead and could see a large, open area where I might make good yardage. I ran into it; no one really had a good shot at tackling me. I discovered that all of a sudden I had open field in front of me with only one guy who could possibly catch me. I don't know that I ever ran so hard in my life to make a touchdown. I was so winded, I could hardly call the play for the extra point.

In our homecoming game with Marsh Valley that year, we were having a difficult time scoring, even though we were deep in their territory. The coach sent me in with a running play off tackle, and when we ran the play, the fullback ran for about eight yards to the two-yard line. (I almost fumbled getting him the ball.) When the coach didn't send Keller back in, I thought the play had worked quite well and so I called it again. We scored our first touchdown.

We beat Malad badly, and the second team was able to play a great deal the second half. I scored a touchdown and moved the team for two additional touchdowns. At the end of the game we had a fourth down and about six yards to go. The coach didn't send in the punter. I was going to call a timeout but decided to act like I was going to punt and told the line to block like a sweep to the right. I must have faked fairly well because I was able to make a first down, and everyone got a real kick out of it since we did not really have a play like that.

The highlight of my football career came in my junior year against Bonneville of Idaho Falls. They were ahead 7-0 with about four minutes to play when the coach put me in the game. They were a very excellent team, and we had been unable to move the ball all day. Keller was very good, but a very conservative quarterback. He had tried only three or four passes the whole afternoon. We had the ball clear back on about our twenty yard line. The first play I threw was a quick pass over the middle for about seven or eight yards. The second play, I threw a pass to the left halfback, circling up the left sideline for about thirty yards. The crowd was really starting to warm up to what was happening. The next play was a screen pass. The line let the defense through, and the fullback waited for me to lob the ball over the onrushing defense. He took off with a real escort of linemen. The play went all the way to the two yard line. I tried a quarterback sneak, and would have made the touchdown, but I fumbled the ball between my legs behind me. Fortunately, the fullback fell on it. I tried two more running plays with no success. On

ATHLETICS

the fourth down, I pitched to the fullback who swept left and barely made the touchdown. Keller came back in to hold for the point-after-touchdown try, and their line got through and blocked the kick. So we lost by one point. That one series did more for my football reputation than anything else I ever did.

The next game was for the district championship against Montpelier. We won. It was interesting, though, that in the second quarter when the score was still 0-0, Coach Oliverson told me to warm up. I warmed up and then went over and stood by him, waiting to get the word to go in, but it never came. I think the coach knew that if he put me in we'd either really go or I'd throw an interception or something, because I was pretty wide-open offensively. He wisely decided not to take a chance at that point, and it paid off.

At the letterman banquet, I was elected to be a captain of the football team my senior year.

I was in an interesting situation the first part of my junior year in basketball. Coach Davis was either playing four seniors and me (which was the usual starting team), or he would insert four other juniors and I'd still stay in. For the first ten games of the year, he platooned this way and would never substitute any other way. I was the only player on the team who played 100% of the time for that period. Needless to say, there was a lot of feeling concerning which team was the better on the floor, and there was a great deal of dissention and jealousy on the team. Later on, Davis started going with two seniors and three juniors for the rest of the year. I was primarily a playmaker and rarely shot over five times a game.

I believe the most I ever scored my junior year was eleven points. We had a poor year, winning only about seven games.

In the spring I started and quit track, as usual. In baseball I became the starting shortstop early in the year. I was the second-best hitter on the team, for a hitting average a little over .300. We played Pocatello one day in Preston; they had a super team. Their catcher played several years in the major leagues a few years later. Their pitcher was a big, well-built Native American. I remember the first two times I got up, he struck me out on big curve balls. He had an extra-good fastball; and when the curve came, both times I almost jumped out of the batter's box thinking I was going to get hit. Then the ball broke over the plate. I'd never seen a curve that broke so far in my life, and he saved it both times for the strikeout pitch after getting two strikes on me with his good fastball.

We went into the last inning, trailing 1-0 and only one player had gotten a hit so far. Our pitcher, Henry Rawlings, had done a very good job, and our coach had had their catcher intentionally walked each time he came to bat. I led off the last inning, and I thought the only way I was going to get on and not get struck out again was to get one of his fastballs. I knew there was no way I was going to hit his curve. I anticipated he'd throw a fastball down the middle for the first pitch. Sure enough, he did, and I lined a single over the pitcher and out into centerfield. We ended up with the bases loaded and one out. While on third base, I thought there was no way I wanted to end up in a close play at home plate with Duke Sims, the catcher, because he was really a physical specimen. The batter hit a soft liner over second base that I thought had a chance of falling in for a hit. I got too far down the line, and when he caught it, I was doubled off third. I felt bad because I had stopped a chance to beat them and had let the catcher intimidate me.

My senior year football season started off with a game at Pocatello. Before the game, as we were walking to the bus, I told Coach Oliverson that I had all the confidence in the world on offense, but thought there were a lot of others on the team that could do a much better job on defense. His response was something to the effect: "Oh, gad, Hart, you big chicken." I think he liked me in there for pass defense because I was far from a great tackler.

I remember getting hit so hard on the opening kickoff that I didn't want to touch the ball for the rest of the half. I played both ways, and not once was I ever substituted. I had full control as quarterback. We lost to Pocatello 26-6, which was a pretty respectable showing against a school that size. I remember I completed several passes in the game and got a good write-up because of it.

Next we beat North Cache 6-0. I scored the only touchdown. The third game was against Marsh Valley, and we beat them 14-0. I scored one touchdown and threw for an extra point. I completed an unusual amount of passes. Most, however, were quick look-ins that were open for short yardage because of where they set up their linebackers.

The fourth game was over at Malad. They led us 6-0 most of the game, but late in the fourth quarter I quick-pitched to

Reid Carlson for a ten-yard touchdown. We knew the extra point was going to mean the game. I threw a pass to Tub Merrill for the conversion and the win.

The fifth game was clearly the most frustrating of the year. It was homecoming, and Snake River was our opponent. We pushed them all over the field and when we got close to the end zone, we couldn't score. We were inside their ten yard line five different times with a first-and-goal and were stopped. They led us 6-0 most of the game because of a dumb interception I threw deep in our territory. In the fourth quarter I finally scored a tying touchdown, but we couldn't convert the point-after.

The sixth game was with Idaho Falls High School. I remember looking down the hall at school when they arrived and could see two 6'5" monstrosities. They had a pair of twins who later went on to play college ball. They played the tackle spots. We almost scored before half-time, but didn't, and were tied 0-0 at that point. The second half they beat us 19-0. In the fourth quarter they had their second team in, and I ran a fake reverse. I had gained about fifteen yards when two defensive backs had the angle on me as I was running up the sideline in front of our bench. The two hit me pretty hard, and when I hit the ground, I had the worst pain I'd ever experienced in my life in my left knee.

The coaches came out and helped me straighten my leg out. The excruciating pain subsided into a more bearable pain after a minute or so. I was really letting everyone know how much I was hurting, too. The coaches went to help carry me off the field, and when I lifted my right arm to put around the shoulders of one of them, I felt some more pain—more of a funny feeling in my right collarbone. They felt it and decided to send me to the clinic to be checked.

Dr. Clair Cutler was at the game, and we got in a car and went to the clinic. I was x-rayed and had a green-willow break on my right clavicle. I was more concerned about my knee, but they said it was okay. While lying on the table in the clinic, two fellow basketball players and friends, Pat Hoggan and Lorenzo Griffeth, were talking to me and seeing what was happening. Pat suddenly fainted, hitting the floor very hard, face-first. He got a bloody nose and loosened his front teeth. I appreciated his sympathy. What you're about to read will sound like too much, but it is the honest-to-goodness truth (as is everything else!). After they put a brace on me for my collarbone break, I got up to leave to go home and found I couldn't put any weight on my right foot. I found that in addition to my injured knee and broken collarbone, I had sprained my right ankle on the same play and hadn't even noticed until later because of the pain in my knee.

The next game was at Bonneville. I wanted to go with the team but felt I couldn't endure the ride with my injuries. We lost something like 40-0. The next week we played Montpelier again for the district championship and I watched from the sidelines as we lost 13-6.

As I review my talents in football, I would say that I was outstanding in leading the team offensively and in play selection. I was a good passer for up to thirty yards, but could not throw well beyond that. My running was average–I had average speed–but I knew where and when to run. Despite my lack of speed I was the punt return man and got more than my share of chances to return kickoffs. Defensively I was the worst tackler on the team, but I guess I was all right at pass defense. I had letters from Ricks College and Utah State University asking me to fill out a questionnaire and return it to them for being considered for scholarships in football. No one came by in person to recruit, but I would never have cared to take the punishment of college football anyway. I'm confident, however, that if an all-league team had been chosen, I'd have been the quarterback. But they didn't do that sort of thing at the time.

In basketball my senior year I got off to a slow start because of my knee, which was slow to heal. I didn't get out of my brace to be able to play until a couple of weeks into practice. I averaged around five points a game for about the first half of the season. The second half of the season I averaged around fifteen points a game.

We started off with a bang, winning all but two of our preseason games. The game we lost was by one point to Pocatello. Malin Davis, our center, had a 1-and-1 free throw at the end that could have won it, but he missed. We also beat West Side on their floor. That wouldn't normally be a big deal, but it was the first time we'd beaten them since the seventh grade and they finished third in state that year in their classification. We also beat Logan, Burley, and Grace, but lost to Brigham Young High in Provo. Their coach, Frank

Arnold, later became head coach at BYU.

We went into a slump and lost the majority of our games in league play, but started playing well as we approached the tournament. We beat Montpelier in the tournament in the first game (they had beat us twice earlier) fairly easily. We were really riding high, and if we won the next night, we would have qualified to go to State. The following morning I got a phone call from a teammate who told me that Coach Davis's mother had been killed in a car crash coming home from the game the night before. This really wrecked our team. Coach Davis's brother, Malin, was our starting center, also. So we went up to play that night without our coach and center and with little desire to play. Despite these setbacks, we played reasonably well, but lost. The next Wednesday with our coach and center back we were beat out of the tournament by Blackfoot (whom we'd beat earlier) in a close game.

We had a lot of dissention on our team that year, also. Ivan always played us five seniors, rarely inserting a junior into the lineup unless someone was in foul trouble or the game was no longer in doubt. Many juniors felt a couple of the seniors were not as good as a couple of the juniors, and they may have been right.

Malin Davis, our center, was only 5'11" tall and had a difficult time defending the larger centers in the league. Steve Porter, a 5'10" forward, was the best offensive player on the team, averaging around seventeen points a game. He had great moves underneath the basket. Against Logan, early in the season, he set a school record of thirty-seven points. Lorenzo

Griffeth, a 6'1" forward was very good on defense and pretty good at rebounding, but was not an offensive threat. Pat Hoggan, the other guard, was pretty good on defense, but was not an effective passer or scorer.

I was the only other player besides Steve who–after the first eight or ten games–would score consistently. I was the second-leading rebounder on the team even though I was only average at rebounding. I was a good passer and below average on defense. I always played very poorly against West Side and Marsh Valley and very well against Blackfoot and Montpelier. I was somewhere in between with the other schools. The best game I ever had in high school was against Blackfoot. I didn't usually shoot a lot back then, but in that game everything I shot seemed to go in. Most all my shots were from the outside. I made ten of thirteen field goal attempts that game, finishing with twenty points. With eight seconds left and the score tied, I hit a long jump shot to win the game and was carried off the floor by the onrushing teammates and crowd. Great night!

I don't think I even went out for track so that I could quit that year. I played baseball and once again was the second leading hitter, batting an average of .300. We won most of our games. My highlight of the season was a bases-loaded triple I hit against Marsh Valley in front of the student body.

I received letters from Carbon College (later College of Eastern Utah), University of Utah, and Utah State, all interested in my playing basketball for them. The nicest, most impressive letter was from the University of Utah and was very complimentary, but I'd never considered going to school anywhere except USU. Evan Sorenson, USU's freshmen coach, came up to talk to me and my folks. When he found out I had committed myself to enter the National Guard for six months on graduation, he told me he would be unable to offer me a scholarship, but asked me to get a hold of him as soon as I got home and that I'd still be able to play.

If they'd have picked an all-league basketball team, I would not have been a shoo-in, but I'd have been strongly considered. The reason I was getting some interest from colleges is that I was a tall guard, which was more unusual then than it is now. I was also just getting started in reaching some of my potential.

During the summers I always played as much softball and baseball as I could. I would play three and four times a week. I generally played shortstop. I also used to keep statistics on everything I did. I could tell you my averages at any time for batting average, runners batted in, etc.

When I got out of the Army, I went down to USU the day I got home to see Coach Sorenson. He was having practice at the time and he gave me a warm greeting and took me to the equipment manager. They gave me everything I needed, plus a new pair of shoes they had ordered for Cornell Green, an All-American at USU. I started practicing at that very moment. I can remember being embarrassed because he put me in a situation where I had to pass to a forward, and I had the ball intercepted the first two or three attempts because I was out of practice after being away for seven or eight months.

The team had played in the varsity-frosh game, but had not yet played a regular game. During the first two weeks I was playing third guard behind an all-state player from Bear River and a player from Ogden High. A week before the first game, Coach Sorenson kicked the kid from Ogden off the team for smoking, and I became a starter.

Our first game was against the University of Utah and the students had to get there early to get a seat, so one side of the field house was completely filled. There was only a trickling of people on the other side. The first couple of times I came down the floor and threw the ball away in attempts to pass to the forward. I was so nervous with 2,500 to 3,000 people watching. Coach Sorenson took me out and put me back in later. I scored seven points, which was second to a kid from Montana who scored fourteen. We lost to a good University of Utah team by some thirty or more points.

The second game was down at Snow College. We were playing a nip-and-tuck game with them the first half and I was having a particularly good game. I had made five out of six field goal attempts and two free throws. About three or four minutes before the half I was just exhausted and needed a rest, but didn't dare ask to be taken out. I felt a little panicky and was looking for an out from the situation.

Under these circumstances, I could tell I was starting to break out into hives. I'd had the hives four other times in my life. Once was when I was very young and had eaten a large amount of gooseberries. Another time was during a basketball practice my junior year. Another was while mowing the lawn when I was home on leave from the Army. Each time I could tell I was getting them because the palms of my hands and

ATHLETICS

bottoms of my feet began to itch for a few minutes prior to my breaking out with them completely from head to foot. I was always completely covered, and my features would all swell up so badly that I would be almost unrecognizable. The itching bordered on the unbearable. Each time I got to the doctor, I would be given a shot of adrenaline, and within five minutes the itching and swelling began to rapidly disappear.

On the night of the Snow College game, when I noticed this process begin, the assistant coach took me into the dressing room so I could shower and get dressed. He was going to get me to a doctor, as I told him I needed to do. He and a man from Ephraim put me in a car and drove me to Mt. Pleasant, twenty or thirty miles north of there. I was lying in the back seat with a blanket over me. When we arrived at the doctor's place and I tried to walk to the office, I found I couldn't even support my own weight, I was so weak.

The next game was with BYU down there, and I didn't get to pay a lot because the coach was still concerned over my hives. I did play a little and made two points. We got beat by over thirty points again, however. At Snow we got beat by twenty, even though we led at the half. Our team was really pretty poor. Our biggest player was 6'4" and wasn't even a starter. As I recall, we had players from the following places: Logan, Tremonton, Ogden, Salt Lake City, Fillmore, Preston, Idaho Falls, Afton, and one each from Montana, California, and Indiana. It may have been the worst freshman team in USU history.

Early the following week after the BYU game, Coach Sorenson called me in to his office and read me a letter from the doctor in Mt. Pleasant. It said that he recommended that I not play any more basketball until I find out what caused my hives because I had gone into shock that night at Snow, and if I hadn't reached medical help in time I could possibly have died. The coach recommended that I see Dr. Worley in Logan and that I stop playing until I did find out what caused the problem. They gave me a thorough check-up and even an EKG but could find nothing wrong.

I was sent to a skin specialist in Salt Lake City and was there given a series of fifty-eight shots to see what things I reacted to. I found that I was quite allergic to grasses and pepper, but nothing that would cause me to get the hives. The next few years' experience taught me on my own why I got the hives. I discovered the causes as I played church or outlaw basketball. Every time I found myself in a situation where I was not enjoying playing, where I was trying only to impress others, or felt a burden of "carrying" my teammates to victory, I got hives. I would feel trapped in a situation that I didn't like and would start worrying. Then I would break down and get the hives.

I stopped playing games for several years when I was coaching and then started again in 1971. Since then I've never enjoyed playing so much and haven't had the hives once. I almost got them once when I got psyched-out in a championship church game, but I finally shook it off just prior to getting them.

I've always felt very bad that I was unable to continue playing, because I was just starting to reach my potential as a player. For the first time, I was really starting to feel like a

ATHLETICS

very good shooter. I know I could have made the USU varsity teams when I was in school. They weren't all that talented after the first five or six players. This is really one of the biggest regrets of my life. I guess I've always tried to make up for that and tried to "prove" my ability to others since that time.

I'm still playing basketball for fun and to keep in shape. A group of men in two wards in this East Logan area at present play ball three times a week from six to seven a.m. It is the nicest group of guys I've ever been associated with. I've never in two years seen anyone really blow their temper, or do any cussing, griping, or fighting which is often associated with playing basketball. Such pleasant behavior is almost unheard of when playing basketball that often for that long a time. Last year our church team won the stake, region, and made it to the final four teams in Rexburg, losing by only four points to the eventual winners. This year, our basketball team went the same route, winning an extra multi-region championship and again traveling to Rexburg to play.

The last years in Soda Springs found me playing on a very good outlaw team that either won or finished second in every tournament and league we played in. Since I started playing church and outlaw basketball, I've always averaged over twenty points a game and scored in the thirties as often as I fell below the twenties. My shooting ability and confidence have developed to the point that, for the past ten years, there have been few, if any, who shoot as well.

One day in the gym, during the halftime of a ninth grade game in Soda, I shot fifteen consecutive jump shots at points all beyond the top of the keyhole. I played one game in Malad where I scored close to thirty points in the first half and the father of one ballplayer told me I hadn't even missed an attempt. When I thought back, I realized that I hadn't. Most games find me shooting from 60% to 70% accurate shots. My favorite shot is a twenty- to twenty-two-foot shot from about a 45-degree angle. As I read back over these past few sentences, I find I have been bragging about my shooting ability, which serves to point out how much I've tried to compensate for not being able to continue playing basketball on the college level.

One year, in 1971-1972, our team of seven players (all good friends like Wally Bennett and Lloyd Rasmussen) won the Soda League, the Montpelier League, and five tournaments, finishing with a record of forty wins and no losses. About twelve of these wins were against very good teams.

I'll always have real love for and interest in athletics, although when I look at it objectively, I realize that it is not really that important in comparison to many things in life–things like family, church, friends, and even government. But the various sports have played a major role in my life and I spend a great deal of time as a participant, a spectator, a viewer, or one who reads a great deal about what's happening in the world of sports.

Update on Athletics written in 2019, age seventy-seven years old

Sometime when I was sixty or so, I was asked to play in the summer games in Cedar City with the best players in that age group from Cache Valley. Lanny Nalder, a PE professor, was the leader of the group and close to the best player–at least he thought so. We had size with Bob Sorenson, another PE professor, Paul Rasmussen, and former Aggie Dave Basinger who all pushed 6'6". We had other good players, too.

We played down there four different years against the best teams from Salt Lake City and the Provo area. There were 1-3 former college players on each of the best teams. It was really good competition once you got past your first game. For whatever reason, Nalder–who usually treated most teammates *with contempt or perhaps not as buddies–seemed to really appreciate me as a player and teammate. It's probably because I didn't shoot too much and passed the ball well. I made sure if Nalder was open I always got him the ball.*

I had become deadly when left alone at the three-point line. Once I hit a few, they came to realize how dangerous I could be, so they'd guard me much closer and shut me down.

In the four years we won the whole thing twice, finished 2nd once, and didn't place at all the other year. The year we didn't win anything, we lost in overtime to the eventual champions with only four players on the court because three of us had fouled out prior to overtime.

I also played in the senior games in St. George a few times. In one game against a team from Denver I hit nine out of eleven three-pointers and scored thirty-three points. I couldn't miss that game. I've had about five or six games in my lifetime where everything I shot went in and you couldn't wait to get your hands on the ball.

Since retiring, I've played a lot of golf. I've bought season passes to Logan River and played almost every weekday. My average score is right at forty-three for nine holes. These past two weeks I've had a thirty-eight and two thirty-nines. That's a little better than I usually shoot.

My best score ever is two over par and I've had two of those. I've had three hole-in-ones. The first was on #4 at Logan River, witnessed by Ken Mitchell and Lynn Janes. My second was on #8 at Logan River, witnessed by my regular golf group (although I forget specific names). My third was at GateWay #16 in St.

ATHLETICS

George, witnessed by Wally Bennett, Brent Nyman, and several others who were there waiting for their turn on the tee box. I've always maintained I'd rather be lucky than good and that's been the case. Most golfers never get one. In our present golf group of ten, only four have had a hole-in-one and only two of us have had more than one. I need to get one more before I die so each child can have one of my hole-in-one trophies to remember me by.

I've always believed strongly in being physically fit. Since retirement, I've regularly gone to a gym and lifted weights, stretched, and when the weather doesn't allow me to golf, I walk the treadmill on an incline. The way I eat I'm convinced I'd have Type II diabetes if it hadn't been for the physical activity I've been involved in.

I think one of the keys to keeping fit is finding something you enjoy doing that is physical. It makes it so much easier to do that way: golf, pickleball, tennis, running, swimming, basketball, etc. Over the years, mine have been basketball, golf, and lately, some pickleball.

COACHING

I knew I wanted to coach at age fourteen and didn't deviate from that interest. Actually, I knew I wanted to be associated with athletics and felt coaching was the only way. But as I look back, I'm sure I could have fulfilled my athletic interests by just participating in leagues and organizations and chosen another profession. I also wonder if I'd have been more fulfilled by being a sports information director, sports writer, or broadcaster. I'm not crying over spilt milk, because I have a good memory of coaching and am happy doing what I'm doing now.

The first time I had a chance to coach was when I student-taught during my senior year of college. I taught two PE classes at Preston, and my old coach, Ivan Davis, turned the sophomore team over to me. We won five games and lost one. The game I felt best about was a game at Logan. We were trailing at halftime, 14-0. I made some critical changes at halftime, and we came back and beat them 21-14.

When I started coaching at Malad, I was an assistant football coach to Ralph Harding, who was the oldest coach in Idaho at sixty-three. He was a great guy and I enjoyed working with him. He was quite old fashioned and still ran the single wing. I've never heard anyone before or since, though, who could give a more inspiring halftime talk. Our season was 5-5 in football.

In basketball I had a pretty good team, but we were short on height and our center was very weak at his position at the start of the year. We were just doing so-so the first half of the year, and at semester time a 6'3" player named Craig Daniels became eligible for the team. His parents were separated and he came back to live with his grandparents. When he began to play, we had a very good team. He really helped our rebounding and defense. He was also a good scorer. The center, Frank Thomas, began to gain some confidence and was helping more, also. We upset the top two teams in the league during the last three weeks of the season.

When we entered the district tournament, we led in our first game against Aberdeen until the last minute-and-a-half when they threw a press on us. We lost our composure completely and lost. They scored seven straight points and won by three. The next night we played Montpelier, who hadn't won a game all year. We trailed the whole game and barely caught up the last minute and won by one point. They had played very well, and we had played poorly again.

The next night we met American Falls, who had won the league. The tournament was being held in their new gym. I figured we'd lose and the season would be over. We played a so-so game the first three quarters. So did they. Our defense really tightened up at the end, and we won by ten points in the biggest upset of the tournament.

We had three days before our return game with Aberdeen and we worked hard on their press. When we started to pull away from them, they threw their press on us again and we bombed them. I don't think I ever had a team handle a press like we did that night. We certainly ended up getting layups until finally they had to stop. We won by over twenty points.

The next night we played Preston. The winner would qualify as one of the two teams to go to state, and the loser was out. We played very well. So did Preston. The game was going right down to the wire. Preston had a three-point lead with about fifty seconds to go when Mel Christofferson stole a cross-court pass and went down to score a layup. A couple of minutes prior to this, our center had fouled out. I didn't have much confidence in our substitute center, so we put in another forward (three) and went to an offense that did not require a center. Preston came down and one of their players palmed the ball. We gained possession. We were into our offense with only a short time to go and the packed house was going wild. Mark Alder (the substitute inserted for the center) drove across the middle of the keyhole and shot an eight-foot hook shot, which he'd never tried before. It went in with eight seconds to go. Preston came down and threw up a desperation shot that was no good. Malad had qualified for its second state tournament in the history of the school.

The next night we played Snake River, who hadn't lost in the tournament and was also going to state. We beat them by nineteen. Saturday night we played our seventh straight game in American Falls for the championship as both teams had lost once. We lost by nine in our first poor game since the second of the tournament.

The next week we went to the state tournament in Twin Falls. Our first game was against Emmett. We led them in a close game until the last couple of minutes, and they won by four. Two nights later, Emmett won the state championship.

The second night we played Moscow, which had the biggest and most talented team in the tournament. They could have beat us nine times out of ten. We played very well. Terrell Harris made ten out of eleven field goal attempts. We upset them by six points.

The final night we played for the consolation championship against Madison High from Rexburg. We played the worst game we played all year and were thoroughly embarrassed. The score at halftime was 35-14. We ended up getting beat by about thirty points. It was one of the most embarrassing events of my career.

In baseball, which I also coached, we had a great team which won seventeen and lost only three. Our best player,

Harris, couldn't play because he came to the Junior Prom drunk. We lost the championship to Pocatello, whom we'd beaten earlier–a school about five times our size.

The second year I coached the basketball team would have been pretty good. We had excellent shooters and the only area we would have had to be concerned about was rebounding. We were 3-2 during preseason. Then I learned that four seniors (all starters) had been drinking. I decided that I wanted to kick two off permanently and suspend two for four weeks and then let them back on. The two I wanted to suspend had been very honest and open with me when I asked them about it and seemed genuinely sorry. The other two had lied and lied, trying to get out of it. But when the two others had owned up to it, I felt we had the goods on them.

I knew what was happening was going to really affect the small community of Malad, so I asked the superintendent if I could meet with him and the school board. They called a special meeting and all agreed it would be hard to handle the four boys separately and we all agreed to kick them off for the year. A few days later the other starter, a junior, came and told me he'd been involved in the same things and that he was getting a lot of pressure to come clean. So I lost all five starters.

We played two reserve seniors and the rest of the players and lost most all of our games by twenty or more points. We didn't win another game. Our last game of the season was against Marsh Valley in the tournament, and we played very well. We lost in overtime. Marsh Valley went on to win the tournament and go to state.

Getting the involvement of the school in the decision turned out to be one of the best things I ever did. The parents (two of them in particular) did all they could to exert pressure for reinstatement, but could find no support from board members, administrators, or the community as a whole. Those two families and one other father the next year were the only people, to this day, who I think were not strong supporters of my coaching at Malad. I realize I wasn't a great coach, but even to this day, I'm thought of as the best basketball coach that Malad ever had. This, once again, sounds like a big statement, but things did go well there and did not go as well in Soda, as you'll see.

The second baseball team I had was also outstanding with a similar record to the first year. The end result turned out the same, too, as we finished second to Pocatello.

We had a very good team my final year at Malad, although we were once again short. (In seven years of coaching I only coached one boy over 6'3". He was 6'4" and was not a dominating ballplayer, at that.) We won every league game except two to Soda Springs and two to American Falls. Those two teams finished 14-0 and 12-2 in league with American Falls losing to Soda twice. American Falls beat Soda Springs twice in the tournament, however, and went to state as the first place team, but Soda won the state championship. We made it to the final four in the tournament and Preston (whom we had beaten each time earlier) really thumped us. We almost beat American Falls once and almost beat Soda twice that year.

COACHING

In baseball we didn't have as good a regular season as we had the past two years, but the end result was better. We beat Pocatello for the district championship on an error in the second extra inning.

When I went to Soda, I assisted in football the first year and was golf coach for five years before quitting to run a drivers' education program. I can't think of anything significant about the football experience or the golf experience. I did feel guilty about taking $200 for coaching golf, when really I was more of an advisor. I enjoyed that duty so much.

The first year in basketball at Soda was difficult. I had a group of players who had never played. Only one was used very sparingly as a substitute. The rest sat on the bench all year. I think I had worse material than I had after kicking off the five starters at Malad. I should also say that I was aware of this when I switched jobs.

We played a very weak preseason schedule and won five of the six games. When we got into the league we didn't win one of the fourteen games. The last three games of the year I could definitely see some progress being made, mostly due to the maturing of Lynn Nelson, our 6'3" junior center. We lost badly the first game of the tournament but the next night we won a game against a good Aberdeen team. The game was filled with a lot of strategy. I think I made more adjustments that directly helped the team that game than any other I ever coached.

The next night we lost in a close game and were done for the year. I might add that toward the end of that year I was getting very discouraged. On the day of our win against

Aberdeen, I had gone to my room on two different occasions and prayed, not for victory, but that we might play well, that I might see that my efforts for the whole year had not been wasted, and that I might see we had made progress during the course of the year.

Our efforts paid off the second year. We scheduled an easy preseason schedule and were 5-1. Then we went 9-5 in our league and finished 3rd. The first two teams finished 1st and 2nd in the state. We also finished 4th in the tournament. This particular team didn't have a lot of natural ability, but had great attitudes. If we had been able to shoot outside like my Malad teams had, we could have won it all. But the only outside shooter I had was a forward who had his leg broken at the end of the football season and missed the entire basketball season.

It was about this time that I started to lose a little of my enthusiasm for coaching. It happened very gradually through the next year, but after this point, I never was as completely involved as I had been the first five years.

My third year at Soda was another pretty good one. We had a very tough preseason, winning only one game. In league play we went 10-4 and finished 3rd for the second straight year. But I was disappointed that we were upset in the third game of the tournament by a poorer team.

At the end of this year I was seriously contemplating quitting coaching. My desire to coach had pretty well gone by this time, but I felt we had the potential to have a pretty good year the next year and decided I'd go one more year and then give it up. There was a period of three straight years with little or no talent after that time, so it seemed it would be easy to quit coaching after the one more year.

The last year was the most frustrating year of coaching by far. The team had been pretty good as sophomores, winning eighteen games and losing four, but four of the five players were still about the same size that they were as sophomores, and they had not matured any more, either. They really hadn't progressed in ability by even 10% since that time. The other starter was just the opposite. He had grown about six inches and had dedicated his spare time to becoming a better basketball player. His name was Reed Thomas. He was a quick, good-shooting, good ball-handling, defensive guard. Reed was undoubtedly the best player I ever coached. His only fault was that he lacked real confidence in his abilities and wanted to do well so badly that he'd press too hard, and it would interfere with his performance (mostly shooting).

There was tremendous jealousy on the team, especially on the part of one forward who had been the best player when the group were sophomores. I had made these two boys co-captains with the idea that it might bring them together somewhat, but it didn't. This was the only team I ever had that had open dissention. Players were taking sides, blaming early troubles we were having on either Reed or on two or three of our other starters. We were 2-6 preseason, 2-12 regular season, and 2-2 in the tournament.

We did play well in the tournament and in our first game of the year. But other than that it was all downhill. We were never bombed out of any games and usually lost within seven points, but that is little compensation. I told the team during the Christmas holidays that I had informed Superintendent Williams that this would be my last year of coaching. I hoped this might get them going and that it would also protect my own image so no one could ever say that I was fired (I wouldn't have been, anyway), or that I was pressured out of coaching. Nothing seemed to work.

Reed averaged twenty-eight points a game for the first six games, and then about half of the teams defensed us with a box zone and a man chasing Reed. He was essentially double-teamed everywhere he went. Even with this defensive pressure he was able to average about twenty-four points a game.

I tried all I could to help Reed get a scholarship, but he was offered nothing concrete. He was invited to try out for the USU team. He made the team and started on the best freshman squad that USU ever had. He played on an excellent JV team, was a starter his sophomore year, and made the traveling varsity squad his junior year. He wasn't invited back his senior year.

I quit coaching as I said I would, and have never regretted it since. I enjoy and spend more time with my family and on other activities, and I get all the athletic outlet I need by playing church ball, watching Mike, and being a spectator. The Logan area and the university setting offer many opportunities to enjoy spectator sports.

I do not feel I was ever accepted as an extra-good coach by the general Soda Springs public. I think, generally speaking, I was considered to have been an average coach. I was a better coach in Soda than in Malad, however, because of my increased experience and knowledge. I'm sure also that my lessened enthusiasm for coaching my last couple of years didn't help. It was the situation more than anything else that was most defeating. Fresh on the minds of the Soda public was the year before–the undefeated regular season, the number-one rating in the state, and the state championship. My teams suffered from the comparisons, whereas at Malad, I followed two or three poor years with two good teams sandwiched around the year when the starters were dismissed.

Timing is extremely important in coaching and politics. Realistically, my second and third years at Soda were two of the better years they ever had. It was the third and fourth best record they had had in a period of fifteen years, perhaps even farther (I checked the fifteen years out in the yearbooks). I coached there longer than most coaches. My four years were tied with one other coach as the longest stretch in recent years (although I think that in earlier years some coaches must surely have stayed longer than that). The three years after I quit, Soda had three different coaches.

Soda never has, to this day, had an "athletic tradition." Year in and year out they have had losing seasons, with few exceptions. My guess is that they have lost at least two games for every one they've won since their inception as a school. I'm not knocking Soda, however, as I really enjoyed living there. I am trying, though, to describe their attitudes and background.

Overall, I think I was a good coach with special strengths in fundamentals, offense, defense, and particularly in rapport with the players. I think my biggest fault was in not pushing players to their limits–particularly in regard to conditioning. We had fun, well-organized practices. I didn't enjoy getting involved in some of the little details in coaching–particularly equipment. When assisting in football, I used to really get bugged with the continual equipment problems.

Coaching was very exciting. It was a very creative outlet. But it was much too involving, particularly time-wise.

PERSONAL PROFILE

I am now six-feet, two-and-a-half inches tall and weigh about 190 pounds. I have large features (lips, nose, ears, etc.). My feet are size 13 ¼ EEE and this has always caused a problem–getting shoes to fit. My eyes are very light-blue with a flower-petal pattern. I've probably received more comments about my eyes than any other thing.

I don't have very long legs (pant inseam is 30), but the trunk of my body is extra-long. When I was younger, I had a protruding mole under my left nostril that I was very self-conscious about. Any picture taken when I was in school generally shows me giving more of a right profile in order to hide as much of this mole as possible. I was needlessly self-conscious of it, for when I had it burned off, no one even noticed–not even Kay, to whom I was engaged.

I've always had a lot of confidence in my physical abilities and have always found it a fun challenge to do something that takes coordination. I have also always had some kind of habit–such as popping my knuckles, picking my nose, chewing my fingernails, and–most interestingly–pulling out my eyelashes. I guess these habits, in themselves, show some nervous tendencies, although I don't look at myself as being at all nervous.

I'm very fun-loving–always looking for the humor in whatever is happening. I'm the guy who is pulling a prank in the office or having fun at someone's expense (more often than not, my own). I enjoy being the brunt of a joke and make myself out to be the clown in most instances. When I was younger, many were attracted to me because of the fun I seemed to be having. I was voted the "most humorous" by my classmates, which was very satisfying to me.

I'm very optimistic, also looking for the good in most all situations. I'm the type of person who would be happy living in New York City, Hong Kong, or some little place like Fairview, Idaho or Cove, Utah. I'd find out what was fun to do in those places and do them. I think I'd be happy if I were a brick layer or a governor because of my attitude. I hope to always keep it because it makes life more enjoyable.

I enjoy people very much. I find them interesting and stimulating to be around, but not to the extent of being a salesperson. I try to avoid negative situations, and at times this

PERSONAL PROFILE

has strained my relationship with Kay (though not seriously) because she has said that I am unwilling to sit down and talk about problems. She's right, too.

I'm always looking for the easy way to do things. I had systems that saved me so much time in the Army that it was a crime. I've found this helpful in my work, though. I usually end up with the most streamlined ways of getting a job accomplished. When I start a project, I have a hard time leaving it alone until I finish. Because of this, many times I will break larger jobs into parts so I can finish a part at a time without feeling guilty or unfulfilled. Writing this history is an example of a job that I hate to undertake because of the momentous time involved in completing it. But breaking it down into sections allows me to do a section at a time and feel better each time I put it down.

Some friends joke about me being lazy. This is partly true and partly false. I try to pace myself so I don't get overloaded, because when I'm overloaded I can't feel good until I get the things accomplished. I generally tackle so many house projects each summer, putting priorities on each item. If I find myself without a job, I can very much enjoy watching TV, reading, or doing some other activity. In fact, I make sure in my planning that I get enough fun time. But I feel that when I take on a project, I probably work at it more feverishly than most, as I find it more difficult to quit for anything.

I have always worked at being well-liked. I've tried to do the things that people would approve of and tried hard not to offend others. I can't help but feel this has been helpful to me in growing up. Standards need not be sacrificed in achieving acceptance.

CHURCH

One of the foremost goals of my parents was to raise their children to be active members of the church. It is also my goal to raise my children to be active members of the church. I have often heard outsiders relate that they plan to let their children decide for themselves, when they are older, what (if any) church they prefer to belong to. This philosophy may be fine for outsiders as it indicates their churches don't mean as much to them. Their churches are made of the philosophies of men, mingled with scripture. But when a member embraces the gospel and grasps the significance of the authority of Jesus Christ over his church and the power of the priesthood, he is unable to feel comfortable taking such a chance with something as precious as his children.

Each member, even though raised in the church, has to decide at some point in time, however, that he feels strongly enough about the gospel to make a total commitment to the church as an active member. When one is required to give approximately 12% of his gross income for tithing, ward budget, quorum dues, fast offerings, and the like; and when he is to devote from a few hours a week to thirty or forty hours a week (as in the case of a bishop) for volunteer work and services to promote some aspect of the church; and when he is also to spend four or more hours on Sunday in his weekly meetings–he must have a testimony of the truthfulness of the gospel. Inactive Mormons are those who never developed strong enough testimonies to give such a commitment to their Father in Heaven and thus have stopped participating because of this lack of commitment. In essence, then, members as well as non-members don't accept blindly. They must find out for themselves if the gospel is true.

I always enjoyed going to church. That was where all my friends were. In my younger years this was the real reason I attended church–other than that my parents made me (but I did not resist). I can't think of any special spiritual experiences I had until I got to be about the age to hold the priesthood. I can remember walking over to the church with Dad and Mark and feeling very important and proud that we were going to church as a family.

I remember that by about age eleven or twelve I had started paying more attention to speakers, and I believe that at this time I started having some spiritual experiences. I always enjoyed passing the sacrament or doing other assigned duties in the priesthood.

At age twelve I had my patriarchal blessing from a very humble, spiritual man named Cash Carlton. I was always a little disappointed when I was younger because my brother Mark's blessing stated that he'd assist in the building up of Jackson County, Missouri, and I couldn't find anything that interesting in mine. In re-reading it now, I can pick out a few significant things that have become of great interest to me. One is that I'll have a great deal of opportunity to preside over the church and another mentions that I will do a great deal of genealogy work.

I was really turned on to scouting under Robert Rust, our Scout Master in the Logan 4th ward. I rapidly made advancements to a "star" rank with fourteen merit badges. A "life" achievement only needed something like eleven or twelve merit badges, but I couldn't get one in the conservation area, so I didn't get the "life" achievement. I was only seven merit badges from an "eagle," but when Mr. Rust wasn't our leader, I lost my enthusiasm, and our new leader didn't motivate me. I didn't have enough self-motivation to go any further in the scouting program.

We were good kids, but at about age ten I often remember giving our teachers and leaders a few problems. I believe there is no more difficult age group than the nine- to eleven-year-olds. This age area always seems hard to handle in class. We had one teacher, actually a very nice gentleman in our ward, who would end up simply screaming at us every week or so. I remember wondering if the plaster would fall from the ceilings when he lost control. His voice was as high as any woman's.

The best training and education I got concerning matters of the church was in seminary classes. I attended seminary every year in high school and really enjoyed it. I learned a lot from my classes. Seminary is one of the greatest educational opportunities in the church.

I had always planned to go on a mission and had looked forward to it. I remember when Mark was twenty and had his farewell. I was administering the sacrament and the bishop asked me during the meeting if I planned to go on a mission also. I proudly nodded, yes. When I met Kay and fell in love with her, I was still thinking about going on a mission, but for the first time I had misgivings about a mission for me. Having gone for six months in the Army and being separated from Kay and seeing the pressures she was getting to date was more than I felt I could handle for two years. Kay told me when we talked about it to go, and she'd be waiting when I got back, but she said she wasn't going to stay home and not date because too many things could change in the meantime. I realized then that if I went on a mission that she would never be there when I got back (not that I don't think she meant it when she said she'd wait, because I'm sure she was sincere). But she was mature and ready for marriage and would have gotten pressured from every returned missionary who knew her. Right then and there I knew it was Kay or a mission, and it seemed to be no contest. From that point on Kay and

I worked toward getting married as soon as we could see it through financially.

My parents handled the situation really great. They both hoped I'd go on a mission, but never put any pressure on me to do so. A few subtle hints, like picking out the colors of a new suit at that time, were the main ways I could tell their feelings. I believe they understood my feelings and could appreciate the decision that I finally made. They both knew Kay well and could see what I stood to lose if I went.

The bishop was also quite understanding. He talked to me and my parents about it one evening. It was easy to see he wanted me to go on a mission. But when I explained my feelings, he accepted them and was very supportive after that. Kay's father probably put more pressure on me than anyone to get me to go. I could see his and others' points of view in directing me that way. Once Mr. Cherrington had again emphasized why I should go but then realized what I had decided, he was very good in supporting us.

At that time, a person had to be twenty to go on a mission. Had it been nineteen, it might have made some difference. I'm not sure, though, as I was pretty well hooked by then.

As I look back, I wish I would have had the experiences in the mission field. It would have helped greatly to increase my knowledge and understanding of the church, and I would have become more committed to the church at an earlier age. I can see the wisdom in not dating until age sixteen for many reasons, and one of them is to keep potential missionaries from falling in love and having that interfere with a mission.

I'm glad that at that time no one had ever said what President Kimball says today about every young man being responsible to serve a mission. I'm sure I would have gone under those circumstances. Marrying Kay was the best thing I could have done, and I'm glad I did. It would have been even better if I could have done both, but I'm convinced it would have never turned out that way.

As I was growing up, I used to regularly get 100% attendance awards each year. The only time I ever missed church was if I was sick, which was very unusual. I don't remember what the requirements were, but I also received a Duty to God award.

After Kay and I were married, we served a while as ward dance directors, which was interesting because that's the program that was the basis for us getting together.

While I attended college at USU, I questioned the church more than at any other time in my life. Everything that is not entirely scientific is questioned and looked upon with much skepticism in a college atmosphere. I never was far from the church, but at this time I wanted to have everything explained. It seemed, at times, that there just was not a scientific explanation. But that doesn't bother me in the least anymore because I realize that God's ways are not man's ways and that man does not have all the answers. There are logical and acceptable answers for everything. As I look back on my life, I can also see that when I had the most questions about the church were the times that I was not living 100% as I should have and I must have been looking to rationalize my actions.

I have had many callings in the church since I got married.

CHURCH

I'll try to remember some of them and my thoughts about each one. I know each responsibility in the church is significant and important and that the programs of the church could not progress if members didn't accept any and all positions. Some positions do lend themselves to more personal growth than others, however.

In the Logan student ward I was a ward teaching supervisor and had the responsibility of calling a group of brethren to encourage them to do their home-teaching and see if they had their home-teaching completed. I referred any problems to the quorum leader.

In Malad I was the teachers' quorum advisor. At that time I really liked that job. Back then, this job wasn't tied into the APYW program and basically involved teaching a lesson on Sunday morning.

In the Soda Springs 1st Ward I was the priests' quorum advisor. This, too, was a Sunday-only type of job at that time.

In the Soda Springs 4th Ward, where we lived for seven years, I was a teacher's quorum advisor again for a while. Then I served as a counselor in the MIA program. (It seemed there wasn't anything significant to do.)

I taught Sunday School for the ten-year-olds for about two months. What a struggle. One boy was particularly impudent and one day I slapped him twice for his misbehavior. At that age, kids seem to need a lot of discipline in order to keep their attention. After this, (though not because of this), I was switched to the seventeen-year-old class. I really enjoyed that age group, more than any other, and that was the best church job I had to that point. I taught that group for two or three years.

I was called to be a seventy in the fall of 1973. I was set apart by Elder James Faust who was a general authority. I purchased the missionary materials. We were to memorize the lessons and go out with the fulltime missionaries. There were only four seventies in our ward, and we would meet an hour early for Priesthood Meeting to study the lessons.

Before I ever had a chance to teach someone the gospel, Kay and I were asked to meet with the stake president one Saturday evening. This was the end of March, 1974. When President Burton told me he wanted to call me to be the second counselor to Bishop Murray Godfrey in our ward, I was really surprised and humbled. The first counselor had been called to be an alternate high councilman, and Keith Nielsen had been moved from second to first counselor.

The next day I was set apart and started a calling that was to last for a year and three months. I have never been humbled more than that before or since, and I served as best I could. I think I went the extra mile in everything I did and never shirked any responsibility. Bishop Godfrey and Brother Nielsen were both truly outstanding and dedicated and I felt I had to do my best to keep pace with them. I felt so inadequate that in the course of that time I read the entire standard works of the church and about six other good church books. I got really involved and loved the people of the ward. I had many truly spiritual experiences. As I look back at this point, I realize that this calling has easily been my greatest experience in the church to date.

For a year-and-a-half prior to this calling I'd had four or five strep throats each year. I had been told that I should have my tonsils out and had even set up an appointment with my brother-in-law, Dr. Perry Roberts, in Ogden to have them removed. I was blessed in my setting apart that I would enjoy good health during my call. I haven't had one strep throat since that time, which has been two years.

The most difficult thing for me to do as a counselor was to extend church calls to those who were semi-active or inactive. I had some real answers to my prayers when making some of these calls. My biggest problem was the Cub Scout program. Within two or three weeks after I became a counselor, three of the leaders asked to be released. I got replacements for them, but they didn't work out. I prayed that I might get the problems resolved. After about six months and several more disappointments and more extensive prayer, I was struck with the answer. I changed Brother Walker from Webelos leader to pack leader and made some other calls. From then on, things went very well in my areas of responsibility. After getting the job at USU, I was released as counselor and replaced by Wally Bennett, which I was really tickled about.

We moved into a new ward, the Logan 27th, which had just been split from another ward two months prior to our arrival. The 27th ward is housed in a beautiful building, the most beautiful I've ever been in. Our bishopric was reorganized about three weeks after we arrived and I was called to be chairman of the services and activities committee. I served there for a year, during which time the two other members of the committee and I organized every party, every service project, and every fundraising project that the youth had. We were also basically in charge of the opening exercise programs. It was a little frustrating to try and keep coming up with new ideas for everything.

I also had to organize a ward youth conference. Just two weeks prior to the conference, I was called to be an alternate high councilman in the USU married stake. In this calling I was an advisor to the two elders quorums in my branch. Later I was made a regular high councilman and was given the stake athletic program to direct. This call as a USU stake high councilman is usually a three-to-five year calling.

My being a missionary hasn't gone as well as I had hoped. I've talked to several non-members and have given a couple of Books of Mormon to prospects, but with no results.

My assistant coach in Soda Springs was J.B. Smith. I asked him if he'd like to take the lessons and he agreed. He had every lesson either in our home or with us at his home. But when he was challenged with baptism, he said he wasn't ready. About four years after that, he joined the church, however. I've got one young man in mind now who has been taking the lessons in our home, also, and I hope he, too, joins the church.

One of the most embarrassing and yet funny things that has ever happened to me occurred as Wally and I and two others were singing "I Need Thee Every Hour" in sacrament meeting a year prior to my being called to the bishopric. We were doing just fine until we got on the last verse, and it sounded to me like the whole song was starting to crumble with the two guys between me and Wally. I kind of stopped singing very loudly so I could listen to what was the matter. At that moment, everyone had either stopped singing or else were singing so quietly that Wally was the only one being heard. This whole impression was developed in just one or two seconds at most, and struck me as being terribly funny. I burst out laughing. I was terribly embarrassed, and I tried to get serious and pick up my part. But then the whole situation got even funnier and I burst out laughing again. I kept my chin down on my chest so no one could see my face and kept bursting out laughing and yet tried to hide it, which was impossible. Fortunately, Wally, with little help from the other two and no help from me, finished the verse and we were able to sit down.

We were sitting on the stand in the choir seats! I was so embarrassed that I hid behind the seat in front of me, leaning my forehead down on the back of it. I tried to get serious, but things were so out-of-hand that I just hid. Earlier that afternoon at practice I had said that this was the best quartet I had ever sung in. The first time I finally gained control after sitting down, Wally leaned over and said, "The best quartet you ever sang in, huh, Dave?"

This set me off again. Halfway through the meeting–for the first time–I gained enough courage to look up over the seat and out at the congregation. The first face I saw was that of our former bishop. He was looking right at me with a huge grin across his face, and I was off again laughing.

By the end of the meeting I got control of myself and the ridiculousness of the whole thing wore off. The one thing I was grateful for was that all this happened in the middle of the last verse. If it had happened earlier in the song, I would have made the biggest possible fool of myself and would probably have had to leave the building in the middle of the song rather than just stand laughing in front of everyone with tears streaming down my face. I'm sure that no one who was in that meeting will ever forget what happened. If I hadn't had a testimony, I may have never returned, myself.

I want to end this section of my life history with some explanation of my testimony for my children and grandchildren. This is the hardest part to write, I find, because it is hard to write down special feelings and try to explain them with the where's and why-for's. The gospel is so important to me. I know a lot will be lost in the translation of my thoughts onto paper.

I want my very special children and all others of my posterity to know that I know we hold membership in the church that Christ has restored to the earth in these latter days. I know that this church is the only church with power and authority (Priesthood) delegated from God and Jesus to men.

The more I study and learn about the church, the more everything fits. The many ministers of other churches who have joined our church indicate that the more they learned and studied, the more they also became convinced to the truthfulness of this church. I have enjoyed such stories of conversions in the three volumes of No More Strangers, by Hartman and Connie Rector.

To those who read this life history who are also having

trouble accepting the gospel, I would encourage you to study, keep the commandments, and pray for an answer. If you desire the truth enough, you will receive a witness of it through the Holy Spirit. The scriptures say that if something is of God and is good and true, it will bring forth good fruit and will grow and flourish. But if anything is not of the truth or is not good, it will bring forth bad fruit and will eventually wither and die. I find this the case with our church. As one sees how dynamic the church and its growth are in comparison with the other churches and their decreasing attendance and changing doctrines, this statement takes meaning. Other churches now look for attractive ways to increase involvement and attendance–modern rock music, endorsed homosexuality, gimmicks for livening up services, and the search for common grounds in order to consolidate with other churches. God is the same yesterday, today, and tomorrow, and his gospel does not change to meet the fads and changing ideas of man.

Too many prophecies have come to pass. Too many signs are now present to deny the gospel's truth just on the basis of logic alone. The Book of Mormon, in and of itself, is a testimony of the truthfulness of the church. Its history of the Native Americans, which has been widely published and scrutinized as it has, continues to be and will always be a beacon of truth and great witness.

My own personal experiences with prayers being answered, some very special experiences my great father has had, and special experiences where the Holy Spirit has been especially strong, all add to this testimony. The testimonies of others whom I admire and respect also have become a part of my testimony and learning experiences.

I would like to relate two special experiences that have always meant a lot to me. The first happened at a time when I was younger. Dad had compiled hundreds of words and their meanings as a hobby and was toying with the idea of putting them in book form for possible marketing. One night as he was in bed, a voice, which he stated was very clear and definite, said that if he ever wanted to get out of the classroom (he was teaching at the time), he should put the definition before the word. Those are not the exact words, but the voice indicated to him the format that he should use for the vocabulary lessons. Dad worked with the book, and in the next few years his business got so good that he gave up his teaching. It is his feeling that he could only have done the temple work he has done (and he has done a great deal of it!) with a flexible business that didn't tie him down such as a teaching job did. He felt this was the reason for the personal revelation.

The second experience (actually two related experiences) was also related to me by my father. These happened in the temple meetings for temple workers. On two separate occasions, which were a few years apart, a member of the group got up during the course of the meeting and began speaking in tongues. After this person was done speaking, another member of the group was inspired to stand and interpret the message that had just been given. The theme of the message in both instances was that the time was short and there was a tremendous importance and urgency to the work in which they were engaged– temple work.

I have heard many such first-hand experiences from great people and could relate them all to you, but it would take a great deal of time and space. I'm sure that if any who reads this is involved in church activities, he will also hear of many such remarkable things.

I have never personally had an intense experience like those mentioned above, but I have perhaps never been as humble as I need to be, either.

My greatest desire is to find my family involved in the gospel of Jesus Christ and furthering the work of the church. This is my testimony which I repeat to you in the name of Jesus Christ, amen.

www.ingramcontent.com/pod-product-compliance
Lightning Source LLC
Chambersburg PA
CBHW040734060526
44119CB00088B/384/J